PARTNER DEPARTURES
AND
LATERAL MOVES

A Legal and Ethical Guide

BY GERI S. KRAUSS

 **LawPracticeManagementSection**

MARKETING • MANAGEMENT • TECHNOLOGY • FINANCE

Commitment to Quality: The Law Practice Management Section is committed to quality in our publications. Our authors are experienced practitioners in their fields. Prior to publication, the contents of all our books are rigorously reviewed by experts to ensure the highest quality product and presentation. Because we are committed to serving our readers' needs, we welcome your feedback on how we can improve future editions of this book.

Cover design by Jim Colao.

Printed in the United States of America.

Library of Congress Cataloging-in-Publication Data

Partner Departures and Lateral Moves: A Legal and Ethical Guide. Geri S. Krauss:
Library of Congress Cataloging-in-Publication Data is on file.

10 Digit ISBN: 1-60442-523-7
13 Digit ISBN: 978-1-60442-523-9

12 11 10 09   5 4 3 2 1

Discounts are available for books ordered in bulk. Special consideration is given to state bars, CLE programs, and other bar-related organizations. Inquire at Book Publishing, American Bar Association, 321 N. Clark Street, Chicago, Illinois 60654.

To Dan and Benjamin

Contents

About the Author

 Geri Krauss is a respected litigator and recognized expert on the complex issues relating to professional partnerships. She regularly counsels lawyers and other professionals in disputes involving partners, employees and their firms, and negotiates and litigates such disputes. Additionally, she defends law firms and lawyers in malpractice, sanctions, malicious prosecution, and contract matters.

Ms. Krauss is also an experienced employment lawyer who has negotiated and litigated a wide range of issues on behalf of both employers and employees, including contracts, restrictive covenants, discrimination and harassment claims, and terminations.

Prior to founding Krauss PLLC, Ms. Krauss was a partner at Herrick, Feinstein LLP, where she was chair of the firm's Professional Practices Group and a member of its Litigation Department, and a partner at Hinshaw & Culbertson LLP practicing in their Lawyers for the Profession Group. Ms. Krauss is a member of the Committee on Character and Fitness for the Ninth Judicial District and served a term as a member of the Committee on Professional Responsibility of the New York City Bar. Additionally, she is a member of the American Bar Association, the New York State Bar Association, the New York State Women's Bar Association and the Westchester Women's Bar Association. She is also on the Board of Directors of the Judges and Lawyers Breast Cancer Alert (JALBCA) and is on the Panel of Arbitrators for the New York State Attorney-Client Fee Dispute Resolution Program.

Ms. Krauss has appeared as a guest commentator on legal issues on television and radio shows, including "Court TV," "Celebrity Justice," "The Today Show" and "Lawline."

Ms. Krauss frequently writes and speaks on topics involving law firms and other professional practices. Her presentations include:

- "The Ethical Considerations When Lawyers Change Jobs," New York State Bar Association, Labor & Employment Law Section, New York City, Annual Meeting, February 2008.
- "Avoiding Liability with Respect to Lateral Partner, Of Counsel and Associate Hiring and Firing," Practicing Law Institute, December 2005.

Ms. Krauss' published articles include:

- "Validity of Nonsolicitation Pacts Among Lawyers Shrinks," *New York Law Journal*, October 21, 2008.
- "New Partners: New Status Brings Change in Approach to Compensation," *New York Law Journal*, February 2, 2004.
- "The Nitty-Gritty on Equity," *Legal Times*, January 26, 2004.
- Partnership Roles Vary Widely From Firm to Firm," *New York Law Journal*, January 27, 2003.
- "Are Law Firm Equity Partners Protected by Discrimination Laws?" *New York Law Journal*, November 19, 2002.

Preface

My path to becoming a "lawyer's lawyer" was purely fortuitous. In the early 1990's, I joined a firm in the midst of trial preparation for what would become a landmark case. Our client was the name partner of a mid-sized New York City firm—a firm which he had founded decades earlier—who left to go to another firm with two partners and one of the firm's largest clients in tow. When he notified his soon to be former partners of his plans, they responded by locking him out and suing him, claiming that he had breached his fiduciary duties to them by the manner in which he left. He, on the other hand, claimed that his actions were mandated by his fiduciary duties to his client. Surprisingly, there was virtually no case law which provided any guidance as to how these two fundamental duties could or should be reconciled. We were about to blaze new ground.

The trial was adjourned and the case instead proceeded to the highest Court in the state. It was one of those rare cases which presented an opportunity to address the merits of public policy issues that go to the heart of the obligations of the legal profession. The Court found the issue to be one that was too complex to draw any hard lines and articulated only the permissible and impermissible behavior at the far ends of the spectrum. To date, those hard lines still have not been drawn.

But the question—what is it that a partner can and cannot do in seeking a new affiliation—is a very practical reality that lawyers all over the country face as they consider leaving their existing firms or find themselves wooed by competitors. And in an economy in which old and venerable firms have collapsed and core areas of business have all but disappeared, the stakes for retaining—as well as acquiring—those partners who continue to have dynamic practices could not be higher. Indeed, in these times, the defection of a key group of partners could well cause a downward spiral from which a firm cannot recover. And if those partners—or the firm they go to join—do something that crosses the bounds of permissible conduct in the process, it is now all the more likely that firms may turn to suing their former partners and the acquiring firm to recoup their losses.

So, what steps can a departing partner or an acquiring firm take to minimize the risk that the bright future they envisioned together does not become their worst nightmare? This book is a guide to answering that question. In my years of advising lawyers and law firms involved in this process, one of the most recurring issues is that the advice as to what to do—and more importantly what not to do—is not sought until the process is well underway and, in many cases, mistakes have already been made. All too often terrific lawyers, who are scrupulously careful in making sure that they know the law and the facts before advising their clients to act, find themselves far less vigilant when they are the subject of the transaction. And they are surprised to learn that what they genuinely thought to be perfectly proper, in fact poses some serious questions. And while a firm may view the disclosure of information it requests from a proposed lateral as necessary and appropriate to perform its due diligence, it might well find itself taking a very different view if it found that one of its partners looking to leave was the one doing the same disclosing to a competitor. The conflicting nature of the duties and interests involved, the fact that the rules are still in their nascent stages, the potentially damaging consequences for a significant misstep, and—perhaps most importantly—the fact the lawyers involved on both sides of the move are not disinterested, all point to seeking advice as early as possible.

While this book sets forth the basic principles, these principles teach that each case turns on its unique facts and circumstances. Negotiating those nuances requires thought and careful consideration of the risks and benefits of contemplated conduct, particularly since there often are no clear answers. One of my great pleasures in counseling lawyers is the unique opportunity to contemplate these issues together with someone who can engage in the same analytical process and jointly arrive at a resolution that makes sense—legally and ethically—to both of us. Another joy is that which comes when clients who have gone to the effort to seek advice and follow the rules are able to knowingly and quickly gain the upper hand in responding to recriminatory allegations levied against them on the way out (usually unjustly and with misapprehension of the applicable principles) suggesting that something they did was improper. And just as frequently, once it becomes clear that the rules were followed, the emotions begin to diffuse and the parties can part relatively amicably. Embarking on a new affiliation should be an exciting and promising time. Ascertaining the rules governing the transition is the first step to making it so.

The Necessity of Evaluating Potential Lateral Partners

I

Once it was the exception for a partner to leave a firm. Now the revolving door of partner departures has been deemed a "modern-day law firm fixture."[1] Driven by the escalating needs of clients whose businesses have expanded exponentially in an increasingly global market, law firms similarly have experienced geometric growth. Highly specialized practice areas have emerged as the law tries to keep pace with entirely new industries spawned by rapidly changing markets and technologies. The lure of a bigger platform and the limits that a revenue model based largely on hourly billing rates imposes have caused attorneys to explore the opportunities available to them at other firms.

For a law firm, a successful acquisition of a lateral partner or lateral group can instantly create a new practice area, add depth to an existing group or breathe life into a withering one. The most sought after laterals bring with them significant portable business which can quickly add millions of dollars to the firm's revenue, with the potential of much more. A lateral who is a recognized expert in a field or who has extensive contacts or experience can greatly enhance a firm's reputation. Synergies with the firm's existing practice areas or clients can multiply the positive impact of the right acquisition many times over.

---

[1]Graubard Mollen Dannet & Horowitz v. Moskovitz, 86 N.Y.2d 112, 629 N.Y.S.2d. 1009, 1010, 653 N.E.2d 1179 (1995).

There are, however, high stakes and significant risks inherent in lateral acquisitions. To attract a highly profitable lateral or lateral group, a firm must make a considerable economic commitment. Not only are there high compensation and start-up costs, but generally it takes several months for the new group and its clients to get acclimated and reestablished before revenue is received, and even longer for any profit to be shown. If the anticipated business does not materialize, what was initially seen as a profit center could turn into a major drain.

Equally serious consequences may result from issues often overlooked in the vetting process. For example, one of the driving forces of the acquisition may have been contemplated synergies because the lateral group had clients in the same industry as that of a significant existing client of the acquiring firm. Once the acquisition becomes public, however, the acquiring firm may learn from its existing client that, as a matter of policy, it does not want its law firm representing any of its competitors. Or, once the new partner advises the largest client he expected to come with him of his new firm affiliation, the client may decline to follow him because of a prior bad experience with the acquiring firm. In an age of Sarbanes-Oxley (which increases penalties for securities fraud and heightens financial reporting requirements) and government charges of lawyer complicity in corporate malfeasance,[2] the ethics and integrity of both the potential laterals and the anticipated clients become critical. The acquiring firm's own competence and reputation can become sullied if it turns out that the lawyers it is seeking to acquire do not share the same standards of ethics and integrity. Personal conduct of the potential laterals, such as prior incidents of discrimination or sexual harassment, alcoholism or drug use, or just plain bad behavior, can also have a serious impact on the acquiring firm.

The acquisition process itself is fraught with minefields that could transform the dream acquisition into a nightmare. If the vetting and hiring processes are not handled in the proper manner, both the departing partners and the acquiring firm could find themselves as joint defendants in a lawsuit brought by the former firm asserting a panoply of claims, such as breach of fiduciary duty, disclosure of confidential information or trade secrets, tortious interference with the former firm's relationships with its clients and/or employees, and unfair competition.

---

[2] For example, a lawyer for Enron's accounting firm, Arthur Andersen, was accused of instigating a seventeen day document shredding marathon via an email to Andersen employees describing how long financial documents need to be kept and when they may be discarded. *See* Thomas, "Called to Account," *Time Magazine*, June 18, 2002; Arthur Andersen LLP v. U.S., 544 U.S. 696, 708, 125 S.Ct. 2129, 161 L.Ed. 2d 1008 (2005).

The best way to avoid these and other pitfalls endemic to lateral acquisitions is to thoroughly vet the potential laterals and make sure that none of the rules that govern the partners' obligations to the former firm are broken. Unfortunately, this is not so easy, as much of the evaluative information the acquiring firm might like to know would require precisely the kind of disclosure that could form a legitimate basis for a lawsuit by the lateral's existing firm. Moreover, the law setting out the rules is still in its nascent stages. Nonetheless, certain guiding principles have emerged which, if followed, can greatly reduce the risks and potential liabilities.

Background:
The Underlying Precepts

II

The principles governing partner departures and lateral acquisitions derive from a combination of legal and ethical precepts. Foremost among these are the clients' right to choice of counsel, prohibitions on restrictions or disincentives against competition by departing lawyers, and fiduciary obligations owed to both partners and clients. In the area of partner departures and lateral hiring, however, these well established precepts do not neatly apply and, indeed, often come into sharp conflict. When faced with such conflicts, the courts have generally tried to achieve a compromise, although one slightly leaning toward protecting clients' interests over partners' interests. At the same time, there is a limit as to how far the courts will bend partners' fiduciary obligations to each other. As the New York Court of Appeals observed in grappling with just such a conflict in its seminal case on the subject, "the loyalty owed partners (including law partners) . . . [is what] distinguishes partnerships (including law partnerships) from bazaars."[3] To the extent it is possible to glean any consensus as to the point of equilibrium, it is to ensure that there is a level playing field for the two firms to compete both for employees and clients and that the client has an opportunity to make a free and knowing choice between them.

---

[3]Graubard Mollen Dannet & Horowitz v. Moskovitz, 86 N.Y.2d 112, 629 N.Y.S.2d. 1009, 1010, 653 N.E.2d 1179 (1995).

5

A. The Client's Right to Counsel and the Lawyer's Right to Move

At the core of the rules which govern lateral mobility is the principle that the client has an absolute right to choice of counsel. This right has been repeatedly sustained as a matter of professional ethics and public policy, and also finds constitutional protection under both the First and Sixth Amendments.[4]

As a means of safeguarding the right of client choice of counsel, the lawyer's right to move or change firms, unfettered in his ability to continue to service clients, has become equally fundamental. The ABA Model Rules of Professional Conduct codifies this principle in addressing "Restrictions On Right To Practice":

> "A lawyer shall not participate in offering or making:
>
> "(a) a partnership, shareholders, operating, employment, or other similar type of agreement that restricts the right of a lawyer to practice after termination of the relationship, except an agreement concerning benefits upon retirement. . . ."[5]

This rule has been adopted by many states.[6]

Based on this rule and the client choice it is designed to protect, the majority of courts have struck down contractual restrictions which, directly or indirectly, prevent or provide a disincentive to a lawyer's ability to move and practice at a competitive firm.[7] Provisions in partnership agreements which

---

[4]Walters v. National Ass'n of Radiation Survivors, 473 U.S. 305, 368-369, 105 S.Ct. 3180, 87 L.Ed.2d 220 (1985) (Sixth Amendment's protection of one's right to retain counsel of his choosing; "the individual's right to ask for, and to receive, legal advice from the lawyer of his choice was fully protected by the First Amendment.") *See also*, Caplin & Drysdale v. United States, 491 U.S. 617, 628, 109 S.Ct. 2646, 105 L.Ed.2d 528 (1989).

[5]ABA Model Rules of Professional Conduct 5.6, originally codified as ABA Model Code of Professional Conduct DR 2-108.

[6]*See, e.g.*:

> *Illinois:* I.L.C.S. S. Ct. Rules of Prof'l Conduct RPC 5.6.
> *Maryland:* Md. R., Cts., J. & Attys., Rule 16-812, MRPC 5.6.
> *Michigan:* Mich. Comp. Laws Ann., MPRC 5.6.
> *New Jersey:* N.J. R. of Prof'l Conduct R. 5.6.
> *New York:* 22 N.Y.C.R.R. § 1200.13 (N.Y. DR 2-108); Rule 5.6 of the New York Rules
>   of Professional Conduct, Part 1200 (effective April 1, 2009).

[7]Pettingell vs. Morrison, Mahoney & Miller, 426 Mass. 253, 256, 687 N.E.2d 1237 (1997) ("The strong majority rule in this country is that a court will not give effect to an agreement that greatly penalizes a lawyer for competing with a former law firm, at least where the benefits that would be forfeited accrued before the lawyer left the firm."). *But see*, Pierce v. Morrison Mahoney LLP 897 N.E.2d 562 (Mass. 2008), in which the Massachussetts Supreme Court revisited Pettingell and held that the same firm's amended partnership agreement,

require departing attorneys to forfeit rights if they leave to join a competitive firm have been held unenforceable to accommodate and protect the client's right to choose counsel.[8] Requirements of various types of payments by a partner on his withdrawal have been similarly overturned because they would have the effect of deterring competition and discouraging a withdrawing partner from serving clients who might wish to have that lawyer represent them.[9] Even strict enforcement of a *per se* rule disqualifying all attorneys in a law firm from representing a client if one attorney in the firm is disqualified has been rejected because to do so would unduly impair the right of clients to select counsel of their choice and restrict the mobility of attorneys.[10]

Recently, a New York court went so far as to hold that nonsolicitation provisions contained in a mutual nondisclosure agreement between firms engaged in merger discussions, which were designed to prohibit "poaching" or "cherry-picking" if the talks broke down, was *per se* unenforceable as an impermissible restriction on the right to practice law.[11]

B. The Fiduciary Duties Owed to Partners

The oft-quoted characterization of the fiduciary duty owed by partners to one another as requiring "[n]ot honesty alone, but the punctilio of an honor the most sensitive,"[12] equally applies to law partners.[13] "The essence of a

---

which imposed the identical adverse financial consequences on all partners who voluntarily withdrew from the firm, regardless of whether they compete after withdrawing, did not violate Rule 5.6. It held that, unlike the prior agreement, the loss of benefits was triggered by the decision to leave, not the decision to compete. California and Pennsylvania have held certain forfeiture for competition clauses to be enforceable. See:

> *California:* Howard v. Babcock, 6 Cal. 4th 409, 863 P.2d 150 (1993) (upholding an agreement assessing costs against any departing partner who competes against the former firm within a specified geographical location).
> *Pennsylvania:* Capozzi v. Latsha & Capozzi, P.C., 2002 Pa. Super 102, 797 A.2d 314 (2002) (enforcing an oral agreement limiting a competing departed partner's recovery of capital contributions).

[8]Cohen v. Lord, Day & Lord, 75 N.Y.2d 95, 551 N.Y.S.2d 157, 158, 550 N.E.2d 410 (1989).

[9]*Seventh Circuit:* Cummins v. Bicker & Brewer, 2001 U.S. Dist LEXIS 2206 (N.D. Ill. 2001) (applying Illinois law).
   New York: Denburg v Parker Chapin Flattau & Klimpl, 82 N.Y.2d 375, 604 N.Y.S.2d 900, 903, 624 N.E.2d 995 (1993).

[10]Solow v. W. R. Grace & Co., 83 N.Y.2d 303, 306, 610 N.Y.S.2d 128, 632 N.E.2d 437 (1994).

[11]Nixon Peabody LLP v. de Senilhes, Valsamdidis, Amsallem, Jonath, Flaicher Associes, 2008 WL 4256476 (NY Sup. Monroe 2008).

[12]Meinhard v. Salmon, 249 N.Y. 458, 164 N.E. 545, 546 (1928). See also, Duane Jones Co. v. Burke, 306 N.Y. 172, 117 N.E.2d 237, 245 (1954).

[13]Graubard Mollen Dannet & Horowitz v. Moskovitz, 86 N.Y.2d 112, 629 N.Y.S.2d. 1009, 1012, 653 N.E.2d 1179 (1995).

breach of fiduciary duty between partners is that one partner has advantaged himself at the expense of the firm."[14] In the case of a lawyer departing from a law firm, these fiduciary obligations continue at least until the departing partner gives the firm notice of his withdrawal.[15] The fiduciary duties that take center stage in the context of lateral movement are those relating to not competing with the firm and not using firm assets for personal benefit,[16] i.e., not to solicit clients or employees for personal benefit, not to use confidential information or firm resources for personal benefit, and not to lie to or mislead one's partners.[17]

C. The Fiduciary Duties Owed to Clients

"Few precepts are more firmly entrenched than that the fiduciary relationship between attorney and client is of the very highest character."[18] Indeed, the relationship between an attorney and client has been held to be "one of the most sensitive and confidential relationships in our society."[19] Its uniqueness is "founded in principle upon the elements of trust and confidence on the part of the client and of undivided loyalty and devotion on the part of the attorney."[20]

To foster this relationship, state codes of professional responsibility impose significant obligations on a lawyer to protect the client's interest and to communicate regularly with the client.[21] These include provisions that require

---

[14]Day v. Sidley & Austin, 394 F. Supp. 986, 993 (D.D.C. 1975), *aff'd*, 548 F.2d 1018 (D.C. Cir. 1976), *cert. denied*, 431 U.S. 908 (1977). *See also*, Reid v. Bickel & Brewer, 1990 U.S. Dist. LEXIS 16451 (S.D.N.Y. Dec. 6, 1990).

[15]Morris v. Crawford, 304 A.D.2d 1018, 757 N.Y.S.2d 383 (2003).

[16]*See*, Day v. Sidley & Austin, 394 F. Supp. 986, 993 (D.D.C. 1975), *aff'd*, 548 F.2d 1018 (D.C. Cir. 1976), *cert. denied*, 431 U.S. 908 (1977):

> "The basic fiduciary duties are: 1) a partner must account for any profit acquired in a manner injurious to the interests of the partnership, such as commissions or purchases on the sale of partnership property; 2) a partner cannot without the consent of the other partners, acquire for himself a partnership asset, nor may he divert to his own use a partnership opportunity; and 3) he must not compete with the partnership within the scope of the business."

[17]*Id.*

[18]Yorn v. Superior Court, 90 Cal. App.3d 669, 153 Cal. Rptr. 295, 297 (1979).

[19]Demov, Morris, Levin & Shein v. Glantz, 53 N.Y.2d 553, 444 N.Y.S.2d 55, 57, 428 N.E.2d 387 (1981).

[20]*Id.*

[21]*California:* California Rules of Prof'l Conduct §§ 3-500 (communication) & 3-310 (avoiding adverse interests).

New York: New York Code of Prof'l Responsibility EC 9-2 (communication) & DR 5-101 *et seq.* (avoiding adverse interests); Rule 1.7 of the New York Rules of Professional Conduct, Part 1200 (effective April 1, 2009).

lawyers to "explain a matter to the extent reasonably necessary to permit the client to make informed decisions regarding the representation"[22] and not to "intentionally . . . prejudice or damage the client during the course of the representation."[23] A "duty to disclose material information can also be derived from the lawyer's fiduciary obligations."[24]

These disclosure obligations can become critical when an attorney decides to seek new employment. The fact that an attorney who has been handling matters for a client is considering changing firms may be viewed by both the lawyer and the client as a very relevant or material consideration affecting their decisions and interests in pending matters. If, for example, an attorney were unknowingly to join a firm which the client viewed as detrimental to its interest or which would result in a conflict of interest, the client could be seriously prejudiced and the attorney would be in breach of his ethical and fiduciary duties to the client. On the other hand, seeking a client's input about a contemplated departure before notifying the firm's partners could well be viewed as a breach of the fiduciary obligations owed to the firm. It is the "overlap, tension, [and] even conflict between these two spheres" that the courts have grappled with in formulating the law pertaining to client solicitation in the context of lawyer movement from firm to firm.[25]

---

[22]*See, e.g.*, Rule 1.4(b) of the New York Rules of Professional Conduct, Part 1200 (effective April 1, 2009); 134 Ill.2d R. 1.4(b); Rules Regulating the Florida Bar 4-1.4(b); Maryland Rule 1.4; Rule 1.4(b) of the Massachusetts Rules of Professional Conduct.

[23]*See, e.g.*, Rule 1.1 of the New York Rules of Professional Conduct, Part 1200 (effective April 1, 2009); Mass.R.Prof.C. 1.3; D.C. Rules of Professional Conduct Rule 1.3(b)(2).

[24]Lang v. Anton, 40 Pa. D. & C.3d 47 (Comm. Pleas 1983).

[25]Graubard Mollen Dannet & Horowitz v. Moskovitz, 86. N.Y.2d 112, 629 N.Y.S.2d 1009, 1013, 653 N.E.2d 1179 (1995).

The Law Pertaining to Client Solicitation

In reconciling the conflict between the fiduciary obligations owed to partners and those owed to clients in the context of lateral partner movement, the courts have tended to focus on four aspects of conduct: (1) timing (whether the communication with the client is post- or pre-resignation), (2) method (whether the solicitation was done properly or was surreptitious, sudden, disparaging, or revealed confidential information), (3) intent (whether the solicitation was to permit client choice or was done for personal gain, such as to enhance the lawyer's ability to get a new position) and (4) scope (whether the solicitation was limited to those clients with whom the departing lawyer had a direct relationship or extended more broadly). While there is general agreement that these are the factors to be considered, where the line is to be drawn remains less clear. Ultimately, however, each of these factors are weighed to achieve the point of equilibrium: whether the conduct allowed the firms to compete with the client on an even playing field and the client was afforded a knowing and unfettered choice.

In the leading case to address these issues, the balance that the New York Court of Appeals enunciated was that solicitation of firm clients that is "nothing more than appropriate client informational service" is permissible, while solicitation which is "surreptitious" and "for a partner's personal gain is actionable."[26]

---

[26]Graubard Mollen Dannet & Horowitz v. Moskovitz, 86. N.Y.2d 112, 629 N.Y.S.2d 1009, 1013, 653 N.E.2d 1179 (1995). In so holding, the court rejected the view expressed by a respected commentator on legal ethics, that "the

Based on these principles, the Court of Appeals set forth "broad parameters" as to permissible and impermissible conduct:

> "At one end of the spectrum, where an attorney is dissatisfied with the existing association, taking steps to locate alternative space and affiliations would not violate a partner's fiduciary duties. That this may be a delicate venture, requiring confidentiality, is simple common sense and well illustrated by the eruption caused by defendants' announced resignation in the present case. As a matter of ethics, departing partners have been permitted to inform firm clients with whom they have a prior professional relationship about their impending withdrawal and new practice, and to remind the client of its freedom to retain counsel of its choice. . . . Ideally, such approaches would take place only after notice to the firm of the partner's plans to leave. . . .
>
> "At the other end of the spectrum, secretly attempting to lure firm clients (even those the partner has brought into the firm and personally represented) to the new association, lying to clients about their rights with respect to the choice of counsel, lying to partners about plans to leave, and abandoning the firm on short notice (taking clients and files) would not be consistent with a partner's fiduciary duties."[27]

While the court expressly declined to undertake what it deemed to be the "unquestionably difficult" and factually dependent task of drawing the "hard lines" defining the large gray area between these two ends of the spectrum,[28] greater guidance can be gleaned by viewing the parameters it did outline in light of the underlying facts of the case.[29]

To begin with, there was no question that there had been a pre-resignation communication with the firm's largest client. The head of the group of

---

public policy favoring client freedom of choice in legal representation should override the firm's proprietary interest in holding its clientele." *See* Hazard and Hodes, *The Law Governing Lawyers* § 5.6:202 (1998). The argument the commentator gives for this view is:

> "The choice that the client is . . . entitled to make when a lawyer leaves a firm is an informed choice. This requires providing the client information about an impending change in affiliation that protects the client against disturbance of its interests and permits it to make arrangements for continued representation informed about the available choices in sufficient time to deliberate and, where a corporate client is involved, to conduct internal deliberations."

The commentator applies these principals to both pre-termination and post-termination solicitation. *Id.* No reported decision has adopted this view.

[27]Graubard Mollen Dannet & Horowitz v. Moskovitz, 86. N.Y.2d 112, 120-121, 629 N.Y.S.2d 1009, 653 N.E.2d 1179 (1995). (Citations omitted.)

[28]*Id.*

[29]The author, together with two of her former partners, represented Moskovitz in the Court of Appeals.

three departing lawyers (and one of the initial founders of the firm) acknowledged that he had advised the client that he was considering joining another law firm, identified the firm, and ascertained whether the client would have any objection if he moved to that firm. He contended that, under the circumstances, this discussion was mandated by his fiduciary obligations to his client: he had had a direct, personal relationship with the client for more than 30 years, had handled the client's tax audits during that period and was in the midst of representing the client in the latest of those audits in which hundreds of millions of dollars were at stake. In his view, if the client had expressed an objection, his obligation not to abandon the client in these circumstances would have trumped his own desire to join the prospective firm.

The firm he was departing, on the other hand, claimed that the attorney had sought to obtain assurances from the client that it would follow him because the prospective firm would not finalize any arrangement with him and his two partners unless the client approved the transfer of its business.

In sending the case back for trial to determine whether "his pre-resignation conduct was nothing more than appropriate client informational service" or "improper solicitation of [the client] for his own benefit," the court tacitly acknowledged that there are situations where pre-resignation communications to clients are permitted.[30] Using the departing attorney's acknowledged conduct as a guide, at least one of those situations is where the lawyer has personally had a long term relationship with a client, at the time of the move is involved in a significant matter for the client, and seeks to determine whether the client would have any objection to the move.

This conclusion is buttressed by the court's statement that "*ideally* such approaches would take place only after notice to the firm of the partner's plans to leave" in describing the timing of such conversations as being after notification to the departing partner's firm.[31] Again, the facts of the case shed light on the circumstances where delaying the communication would be detrimental to the client. The three departing partners in this case had intended to remain at the firm for 60 days after they advised the firm of their resignation so as to ensure a smooth transition and continue the tax audit.[32] Instead, what happened was that when they came to work six days after they had advised the firm of their intentions, they were greeted by locked gates, a guard and a process server.[33] In sending the case back for trial, the court suggested that such a reaction (or the reasonable anticipation of one) might justify pre-resignation notification.

---

[30]Graubard Mollen Dannet & Horowitz v. Moskovitz, 86. N.Y.2d 112, 629 N.Y.S.2d 1009, 1014, 653 N.E.2d 1179 (1995).

[31]*Id.*, 629 N.Y.S.2d at 1013. (Emphasis added.)

[32]Record on Appeal, Graubard Mollen Dannet & Horowitz v. Moskovitz, pp. 64-65.

[33]*Id.*, at 64.

While not discussed by that (or any other) court, in practice the propriety of pre-resignation notification discussions has been raised by departing attorneys in other situations. The issue is perhaps most acute where the search for a new affiliation has been client driven—either because the client wanted to continue to be represented by the partner, but was unhappy with the firm, other partners, or the breadth of services available at the firm. Under such circumstances, the partner may reasonably want (and the client may reasonably expect) an opportunity to discuss proposed new affiliations with the client before making a decision. Indeed, the client may even want an opportunity to meet with attorneys in the new firm. Given the client's expressed unhappiness, the rationale enunciated by the courts for preventing such a meeting—i.e., fair competition—is hardly compelling. Similar considerations may arise where clients are long-time personal friends. Whether a court adopting the New York rule might agree that these situations justify such discussions or meetings is an open question.

An Illinois appellate court[34] set forth its own formulation of the parameters of solicitation:

> "While lawyers who are planning to leave a firm may take preliminary, logical steps of obtaining office space and supplies, they may not solicit clients for their new venture.
>
> "The lawyers may not solicit the firm's clients on company time nor may they use the firm's resources to establish their own, competing firm, particularly until proper notice has been given.
>
> "On the other hand, the current firm has a duty not to interfere with the departing attorneys' continued right to practice law. . . . [I]t is not improper for the lawyer to notify the client of his impending departure provided that he makes it clear that legal representation is the client's choice."[35]

Unlike the New York court, the Illinois court did not expressly acknowledge the propriety of any pre-resignation notification. That issue, however, was not squarely presented as the improper conduct the Illinois court found had occurred went well beyond mere pre-resignation notification. Rather, the departing lawyers were found to have "actually solicited the [client's] business, secured a commitment from [the client] for future business and obtained financing based on that commitment."[36] The conduct included "using

---

[34]Dowd & Dowd, Ltd. v. Gleason, 352 Ill. App.3d 365, 287 Ill. Dec. 787, 816 N.E.2d 754 (2004).

[35]*Id.*, 816 N.E.2d at 793-794.

[36]*Id.*, 816 N.E.2d at 797. The court also found that there were additional breaches of fiduciary duty in the manner in which the partners departed.

confidential records in preparation for taking [the client] with them to the new firm," making sure "the service lists were up to date and the mailings lists were with them so that they could notify counsel of substitution of attorney," "update[ing] and download[ing] the [client's] service lists and mailing labels to disks" and taking the service lists to the new firm immediately upon their departure.[37] The court's focus was on the facts that the departing partners engaged in this conduct for their own personal benefit and that the manner in which they secured the business precluded the client from making a "free and unfettered choice" as to whether to keep its business at the old firm.[38] Notably, the court reached this conclusion notwithstanding the fact that the departing attorney had been the primary person handling the account for 13 years and the client's principal testified that he would not have permitted the existing firm to have continued to handle the account without the departing partner.[39] Even in the face of such facts, the court indicated that proper conduct would have been to have given the existing firm "time to attempt to salvage its long-standing business relationship," by perhaps "offering more attractive fee arrangements (no fees for research, no second chairs at trial, and lower hourly rates . . . usually accorded government bodies)."[40] This ruling (and the $2.5 million judgment the court affirmed) demonstrates just how far the courts will go to ensure an opportunity to compete.

While it is generally accepted that client solicitation is permitted (and, indeed, expected) once the departing partners give notice to the existing firm of their impending departure, the fairness of that solicitation remains the dividing line between proper and improper conduct.[41] Fairness is measured by timing, manner, and content.[42] The closer the solicitation follows within minutes or hours of the notice of departure, the more likely it is that a court will find that the solicitation was unfair.[43] This is particularly so if the departing partners had consent forms to change counsel and authorizations to move files all prepared and ready to go at the moment of notification and sent them out immediately.[44] In person or telephone solicitations are frowned upon and are prohibited in some jurisdictions because they are viewed as creating more

---

[37]*Id.*, 816 N.E.2d at 800.

[38]*Id.*, 816 N.E.2d at 802.

[39]*Id.*, 816 N.E.2d at 801.

[40]*Id.*, 816 N.E.2d at 802.

[41]Meehan v. Shaughnessy, 404 Mass. 419, 535 N.E.2d 1255, 1263 (1989).

[42]ABA Comm. on Ethics and Prof'l Resp., Informal Opinion 1457 (April 29, 1980).

[43]In Florida, a court enforced an employment agreement requiring associates to wait five days before soliciting clients to allow ample time to afford the firm an equal opportunity to compete. Miller v. Jacobs & Goodsman, P.A., 699 So.2d 729, 734 (Fla. App. 1997).

[44]Meehan v. Shaughnessy, 404 Mass. 419, 535 N.E.2d 1255, 1263 (1989).

pressure on clients to consent immediately than would be by letter solicitations, especially if the clients are unsophisticated.[45] Similarly, the departing partners should not use firm resources or confidential information for client solicitation, nor should they solicit clients while on firm premises or firm time. In addition, any solicitation should make clear to clients their available choices. The American Law Institute defines those choices as:

> "Client-lawyer relationships with law firms. Many lawyers practice as partners, members, or associates of law firms. . . . Should the lawyer leave the firm, the client may choose to be represented by the departing lawyer, the lawyer's former firm, or both."[46]

Going to an entirely different lawyer or firm is another choice. Neither the firm nor the departing partners should disparage each other or their ability to continue to represent the client.[47]

---

[45]*See, e.g., Formal Advisory Opinion:* The State Bar of California Standing Committee on Prof. Resp. and Conduct, Formal Op. 1985-86.

> "Similarly, members of the State Bar are prohibited from communicating with clients in person, by telephone, or through agents acting on their behalf, in an attempt to influence the decision of the client with respect to the choice of counsel (Rule 2-101(B) and (C).) Nevertheless, if the client directs inquiries to any of the attorneys involved in the dissolution or withdrawal to obtain information necessary to make an informed choice, the lawyers have an obligation to answer these questions truthfully and accurately, bearing in mind that it is the interests of the client which govern and not the advancement of the attorney's interest in that choice."

[46]American Law Institute, Restatement of the Law Governing Lawyers, § 26, Comment h (Tent. Draft No. 5, 1992).

[47]In Meehan v. Shaughnessy, 404 Mass. 419, 535 N.E.2d 1255, 1263 (1989), the court found that the departing attorneys breached their fiduciary duty based on the use of certain tactics in acquiring client consent to transfer cases to the new firm. Specifically, the attorneys prepared authorization letters for removal of files on the old firm's letterhead, sent the letters, and began communicating with clients as soon as the attorneys gave notice. Further, the attorneys were secretive about which clients they intended to take by delaying response to a request for the list of clients they intended to solicit for two weeks until after authorizations had been received from a majority of the clients. The attorneys also included comments in the letter sent to the clients that were unfairly prejudicial to the existing firm. In Lampert, Hausler & Rodman, P.C. v. Gallant, 2005 WL 109522 (Super. Ct. Mass. 2005), *rev'd and remanded,* 67 Mass. App. Ct. 1103 (2006), *on remand,* 2007 WL 756432 (Super. Ct. Suffolk 2007), a recent Massachussetts trial judge, "reluctantly" distinguished Meehan and disregarded a special jury verdict he deemed advisory which had found a breach of fiduciary duty by a departing partner and associate of a three shareholder firm. The key act in question was the mailing of letters to 194 clients advising them of the new firm and inviting them to transfer their business to the new firm on letterhead with the new firm name but at the existing firm's address. The letters were mailed on the day before a holiday knowing that the letters would not be delivered until two days later when they planned to (and did) give notice. It held that even though the two lawyers were, in the words of Meehan, " 'ready to

To ensure that these rules are met, the preferred method of notification of the departure and presentation of the choices of representation is a joint letter to the client.[48] An informal opinion of the ABA Committee on Ethics and Professional Responsibility sets the following criteria for such joint notification: that the letter (1) be mailed; (2) be sent only to persons with whom the lawyer had an active lawyer-client relationship immediately before the change in the lawyer's professional association; (3) be clearly related to open and pending matters for which the lawyer had direct professional responsibility to the client immediately before the change; (4) be sent promptly after the change; (5) does not urge the client to sever a relationship with the lawyer's former firm and does not recommend the lawyer's employment (although it indicates the lawyer's willingness to continue responsibility for the matters); (6) makes it clear that the client has the right to decide who will complete or continue the matters; and (7) is brief, dignified, and not disparaging of the lawyer's former firm.[49]

Florida is one state that has adopted a specific Rule of Professional Conduct relating to contact with clients upon a lawyer's departure. Rule 4-5.8, which sets forth the "Procedures For Lawyers Leaving Law Firms And Dissolution Of Law Firms" provides in this regard:

---

move' the instant they gave notice to their partners," they had not contacted any client before their resignation, did not send out the letters on the existing firm's letterhead, and the content of the letters were neither one-sided nor prejudicial. The Appeals Court reversed, but on the grounds that the judge erred by nullifying the special jury verdict. In so doing, however, the Appeals Court held that the "evidence amply supported the jury's verdict with respect to Gallant's liability for breach of fiduciary duty." It remanded the case for the trial court to address damages.

[48]*Informal Advisory Opinion:* ABA Comm. on Ethics and Prof'l Responsibility, Informal Op. 1457.

[49]*See, e.g., Formal Advisory Opinion:* The State Bar of California Standing Committee on Prof. Resp. and Conduct, Formal Op. 1985-86.

> "To the extent practical, the law firm and attorneys involved in the dissolution or withdrawal should attempt to provide a joint notice to the clients regarding the change. The notice should identify the withdrawing attorneys, in what field the withdrawing attorneys will be practicing law[] and the name, address, and telephone number of the leaving attorneys. This joint statement may also include information as to whether the former firm will continue to handle similar legal matters. Consistent with their obligations, the attorneys should advise the clients as to who will be handling ongoing legal work during the transition period. In addition, the attorneys are required to inform the client of the client's right to select either the former firm, the withdrawing attorneys, or another lawyer, to handle their legal matters in the future. The client should be advised of the client's right to have all files, papers, and property delivered either to the client, or to whomever the client wishes to continue to handle the legal affairs. (Academy of California Optometrists, Inc. v. Superior Court, 51 Cal. App.3d 999 (1975); Bar Association of San Francisco Formal Ethics Opinion 1984-l; Los Angeles County Bar Association Ethics Opinion 330 (1972).)"

"(c) Contact With Clients.

(1) *Lawyers Leaving Law Firms*. Absent a specific agreement otherwise, a lawyer who is leaving a law firm shall not unilaterally contact those clients of the law firm for purposes of notifying them about the antici- pated departure or to solicit representation of the clients unless the lawyer has approached an authorized representative of the law firm and attempted to negotiate a joint communication to the clients concerning the lawyer leaving the law firm and bona fide negotiations have been un- successful."

"(d) Form for Contact With Clients.

(1) *Lawyers Leaving Law Firms*. When a joint response has not been suc- cessfully negotiated, unilateral contact by individual members or the law firm shall give notice to clients that the lawyer is leaving the law firm and provide options to the clients to choose to remain a client of the law firm, to choose representation by the departing lawyer, or to choose repre- sentation by other lawyers or law firms."[50]

Given the strong preference for a joint letter and the safeguards it ensures against claims of impropriety to all parties, the existing firm and the departing partners are well advised to try and set aside their differences for this pur- pose. However, where a joint letter is not possible or practical, the same cri- teria should be followed in a letter sent by the departing partner or the firm.[51]

Where the partner's departure from the old firm does not take place im- mediately after notification and the departing partner remains at the old firm

---

[50]With respect to "Nonresponsive Clients," Florida Rule 4-5.8 further provides:

"(1) *Lawyers Leaving Law Firms*. In the event a client fails to advise the lawyers and law firm of the client's intention in regard to who is to provide future legal services when a lawyer is leaving the firm, the client shall be considered as re- maining a client of the firm until the client advises otherwise."

"(2) *Dissolution of Law Firms*. In the event a client fails to advise the lawyers of the client's intention in regard to who is to provide future legal services when a law firm is dissolving, the client shall be considered as remaining a client of the lawyer who primarily provided the prior legal services on behalf of the firm until the client advises otherwise."

[51]*Id.*:

"If the involved attorneys are unable or unwilling to provide joint notice, each has the obligation and the right to communicate with the client in conformance with the guidance provided by this opinion. Unfortunately, law firm dissolutions or attorney withdrawals are often fraught with acrimony and accusations of wrongdoing. However, in the context of advising clients of these changed cir- cumstances, lawyers must act professionally by subliming their own feelings for the benefit of their clients."

for a transition period, some limitations have been placed on the departing partner's solicitation efforts. Even though the fiduciary relationship between partners terminates on notice of withdrawal,[52] that still does not mean that the departing lawyer can use firm time or resources during the post-notification period to engage in efforts to solicit the client for the acquiring firm.[53]

The acquiring firm should take an active role in ensuring that the potential lateral does not violate these rules. Failure to do so may well result in claims against the acquiring firm, such as tortious interference with the prior firm's clients or aiding and abetting the lateral's breach of fiduciary duty. Such claims can be based either on the acquiring firm's own complicity in violations by the lateral or as a direct result or the firm's own conduct. To protect against such claims, the acquiring firm should make sure that the potential lateral is well acquainted with the rules relating to client solicitation from the very beginning of the discussions. Moreover, before the lateral actually commences work at the acquiring firm:

- ◆ The acquiring firm should not engage in any solicitation efforts or seek any assurances that any client will follow the potential lateral.
- ◆ The acquiring firm should not contact, speak to, meet with, or seek references from the anticipated clients.
- ◆ The acquiring firm should not provide the lateral with any indicia of the new affiliation, such as letterhead, business cards, brochures, or other materials which could be used for purposes of solicitation.
- ◆ The acquiring firm should not activate e-mail or voicemail until after the lateral commences work.
- ◆ The acquiring firm should not discuss the potential acquisition with any existing clients (including any clients who may be jointly represented) or seek any conflict waivers.

---

[52]Morris v. Crawford, 304 A.D.2d 1018, 757 N.Y.S.2d. 383, 386 (2003).

[53]*See* Adler, Barish, Daniels, Levin and Creskoff v. Epstein, 482 Pa. 416, 393 A.2d 1175 (1978), *cert. denied*, 442 U.S. 907 (1979), in which the court held that the departing attorneys' actions were improper where they used the offices for nine days after notification of departure and used time to procure business for new firm, made contact with the client both by phone and in person, mailed form letters to discharge the old firm including a new retainer. Moreover, in Wenzel v. Hopper & Galliher, P.C. 779 N.E.2d 30, 46-48 (Ind. App. 2002) and 830 N.E.2d 996, 998-1002 (Ind. App. 2005), the court found that "secret solicitation" by a departing partner was improper even after it had been agreed that he would seek new employment but would continue to work for the firm and receive full salary while he looked for a new position. He had remained working for the firm for three months, during which time the solicitations had occurred, and only gave the firm notice of the date he was actually leaving one day before his intended departure.

The Law Pertaining to Acquisition of a Group of Laterals

IV

The law applicable to solicitation of partners and employees differs from that relating to client solicitation. As explained in the leading and most quoted case to address the issue:

> "[T]he fiduciary restraints upon a partner with respect to client solicitation are not analogous to those applicable to employee recruitment. By contrast to the lawyer-client relationship, a partner does not have a fiduciary duty to the employees of a firm which would limit his duty of loyalty to the partnership. Thus, recruitment of firm employees has been viewed as distinct and 'permissible on a more limited basis than . . . solicitation of clients.' "[54]

The difference, however, is more one of timing than prohibition. The rules against restraint of competition with respect to clients equally preclude restraint of competition with respect to personnel.[55] The client can only be completely free to choose to follow a departing partner if the lawyer has the capability to serv-

---

[54]Gibbs v. Breed, Abbott & Morgan, 271 A.D.2d 180, 710 N.Y.S.2d 578, 582-583 (1st Dep't 2000). (Citations omitted).

[55]*Id.* See also, Jacob v. Norris, McLaughlin & Marcus, 128 N.J. 10, 607 A.2d 142, 153 (1992).

ice the client at the acquiring firm. Thus, the client's right to counsel can only be protected if lawyers are able to take with them the other lawyers who have played an active and important role in the client's affairs.[56]

With the absence of any competing fiduciary obligation, the partner's fiduciary duty to the firm generally precludes solicitation of employees until that fiduciary duty has ceased, i.e. once the departing partner has notified the firm of his withdrawal.[57] It also precludes the departing partner from providing confidential firm data to the acquiring firm—at any time—in connection with that recruitment.[58]

A New York appellate court has held that confidential data includes individualized compensation figures (including bonuses), annual billable hours, and the rates at which the firm billed these employees out to their clients. It reasoned that this was information obtained from the firm's personnel files to which the departing partner had unique access as a partner and was not otherwise publicly available.[59] Indeed, the court went so far as to deem this information "privileged."[60] According to the court, the receipt of this informa-

---

[56]*New Jersey:* Jacob v. Norris, McLaughlin & Marcus, 607 A.2d 142, 153 (1992).

New York: Graubard Mollen Dannet & Horowitz v. Moskovitz, 86. N.Y.2d 112, 629 N.Y.S.2d 1009, 1012-1013, 653 N.E.2d 1179 (1995); Gibbs v. Breed, Abbott & Morgan, 271 A.D.2d 180, 710 N.Y.S.2d 578, 589 (1st Dep't 2000) (dissenting opinion); *See* Nixon Peabody LLP v. de Senilhes, Valsamdidis, Amsallem, Jonath, Flaicher Associes, 2008 WL 4256476 (NY Sup. Monroe 2008).

[57]*See, e.g.*: Morris v. Crawford, 304 A.D.2d 1018, 757 N.Y.S.2d 383, 386 (2003); Gibbs v. Breed, Abbott & Morgan, 271 A.D.2d 180, 710 N.Y.S.2d 578, 583 (1st Dep't 2000); Bayer v. Bayer, 215 A.D. 454, 478-479, 214 N.Y.S. 322 (1st Dep't 1926) (Fiduciary duty which one partner owes to another may cease even before an actual dissolution if notice of an intent to dissolve the partnership has already been given and if the parties understand and intend that the firm be dissolved); Weiser LLP v. Coopersmith, 2008 WL 2200233, *1 (1st Dep't 2008) (Prima facie claims for breach of fiduciary duty were made out based on the former partners having engaged in acts, prior to their voluntary withdrawal from an accounting firm, that conflicted with the firm's interests, including using its staff and equipment to set up their new firm and soliciting its clients and employees to follow them to their new firm). *But see*, Appleton v. Bondurant & Appleton, P.C., 68 Va. Cir. 208, 2005 WL 3579087 *19 (Va. Cir. Ct. 2005), (No breach of fiduciary duty where an attorney discussed the possibility of starting a new law firm with two of his existing law firm's employees before he told the firm that he was leaving, where these discussions took place after office hours and away from the law firm's offices); Kopka, Landau & Pinkus v. Hansen 874 N.E.2d 1065, 1071, 1072 (Ind. App. 2007) (An attorney planning to depart did not breach any duty of loyalty by questioning firm employees about their desire, if any, to leave the firm and work for his planned new firm in the future and gathering information about their salary requirements; these acts were deemed to be "preparing to compete" but not "actively and directly competing with [the firm] while still employed there."

[58]Gibbs v. Breed, Abbott & Morgan, 271 A.D.2d 180, 710 N.Y.S.2d 578, 582-583 (1st Dep't 2000) (obligations with respect to confidential information do not cease).

[59]*Id.*

[60]*Id.*, 710 N.Y.S.2d at 584.

tion gave the acquiring firm the "ability to tailor its offers and incentives to recruits."[61] Moreover, the court was concerned that the acquiring firm was made aware of the specific employees who were targets, while the existing firm was not, thereby prejudicing the existing firm's efforts "to retain their associates and support staff."[62]

Although it found pre-resignation solicitation of employees to be a breach of a partner's fiduciary duty to the firm, the court expressly held that pre-resignation solicitation of one's partners to make a joint move is not.[63] It held this to be the case even where the solicitation includes active encouragement by one partner of another initially reluctant partner.[64] The reason for this once again harkens back to the competing principle of the attorney's right to move. As the court stated:

> "[T]he 'solicitation' of one's own partners to make a joint move simply does not qualify as a breach of fiduciary duty. . . . The fact that one partner conceived of the move first and approached the other with the idea, or even convinced an initially content colleague to embark upon a joint departure, cannot change the attorneys' right to leave their firm."[65]

In finding that partners can secretly solicit other partners to move, but not associates, the court endorsed a practical reality: partners who have established a practice together and developed clients together are going to move as a unit. Indeed, given the complexity of most practice areas, more than one partner in the group may have a critical role to play in client relationships. The rationale the court enunciated for permitting pre-resignation partner solicitation, however, should equally apply to associates as a partner may rely heavily on one or more associates he has trained to service the client. The court further did not explain why this rationale necessitates permitting the pre-resignation collaboration between partners (but not associates) at a time when the fiduciary duty of a partner not to compete with the partnership is still extant. If anything, soliciting partners to leave jointly is far more likely to be competitively damaging to the firm than the solicitation of associates.

---

[61]*Id.*, 710 N.Y.S.2d at 583. Due to the specificity and individualized nature of the information, the court rejected the dissent's contention that the financial information provided was not confidential because of the publication of some information regarding profits and salaries in professional publications and because some of it was given to headhunters. 710 N.Y.S.2d at 583.

[62]*Id.*, 710 N.Y.S.2d at 584.

[63]*Id.*, 710 N.Y.S.2d at 582. *Compare*, Graubard Mollen Dannet & Horowitz v. Moskovitz, 86 N.Y.2d 112, 629 N.Y.S.2d 1009, 653 N.E.2d 1179 (1995) (in which there was no discussion of the issue of partner solicitation despite the fact that three partners left together).

[64]Gibbs v. Breed, Abbott & Morgan, 271 A.D.2d 180, 710 N.Y.S.2d 578, 580 (1st Dep't 2000).

[65]*Id.*, 710 N.Y.S.2d at 588.

The illogic of the court's holding becomes more apparent given its further rejection of a claim of breach of fiduciary duty where the pre-resignation collaboration by partners was to plan a group departure which was intended to and necessarily would decimate the firm's entire trusts and estates department. Permitting such activity completely undercuts the court's own rationale for precluding pre-resignation solicitation of associates in the group or disseminating information concerning them, i.e., that "[o]nce the firm is notified of the partners' planned withdrawal, both the firm and the departing partners are on equal footing in competing for these employees; the departing partners no longer have any unfair advantage."[66] In reality, by merely delaying the partners' ability to speak to the associates until after the partners revealed their plan will not place the existing firm on an "equal footing." If every partner in the group plans to leave, the associates in the group (who would likely be the ones they want to take) will have no one with whom to work. Moreover, with the entire group leaving, it will be virtually impossible for the existing firm to continue to service or compete for any of the firm's trust and estates clients. Indeed, a separate opinion concurring in this result so recognized:

> "The observation of the trial court that plaintiffs' joint departure 'denuded' [the firm's] trusts and estates department is irrelevant to the issue of breach of fiduciary duty. Where a department of a law firm contains two active partners, a few associates and support staff, a decision by the two partners to withdraw from the firm will of necessity 'denude' the department, and may indeed even 'cripple' it, at least temporarily."[67]

To conclude that even concerted activity by partners to raid or appropriate a sufficient proportion of the staff and the firm's principal customers so that the former employer's business is crippled severely does not constitute a breach of fiduciary duty—particularly in the face of the finding that there was a breach of fiduciary duty in connection with giving the acquiring firm a competitive edge in hiring the associates—departs significantly from the law applicable to every other business or profession.[68]

---

[66]*Id.*, 710 N.Y.S.2d at 589.

[67]*Id.*, 710 N.Y.S.2d at 589. In so holding, the court noted that the court in the leading case of Graubard Mollen Dannet & Horowitz v. Moskovitz, 86 N.Y.2d 112, 629 N.Y.S.2d. 1009, 653 N.E.2d 1179 (1995), had made no mention of any breach of fiduciary duty in the joint movement of three tax partners who serviced the firm's largest client. That issue, however, was not before the *Graubard* court on the appeal. Gibbs v. Breed, Abbott & Morgan, 271 A.D.2d 180, 710 N.Y.S.2d 578, 588-589 (1st Dep't 2000). Moreover, in *Graubard*, the departure did not leave the firm without a tax department. One partner and all of the associates remained.

[68]*See generally*, Duane Jones Co. v. Burke, 306 N.Y. 172, 117 N.E.2d 237 (1953).

In a recent New York case, a trial judge questioned whether the New York appellate court in *Gibbs*[69] really intended to draw a clear distinction between partners and associates for purposes of pre-departure recruitment, and suggested that a rule more consonant with New York law in other contexts would be that proposed by the American Law Institute and the Philadephia Bar Association, i.e. that a departing partner is free to solicit at-will employees and/or multiple employees unless such solicitation is part of a plan to cripple or destroy the firm business or interferes with an existing contract.[70]

Indeed, other courts have not exempted attorneys from responsibility where their actions were designed to seriously impact their existing firm—at least when fiduciary duties had been violated in the process.[71] In Illinois, for example, the court held that the former partners breached their fiduciary duties in the manner in which they left the firm by, among other things, "arranging for the mass exodus of firm employees."[72] In addition, the California Supreme Court found liability where the departing lawyers engaged "in unlawful and unethical conduct in mounting a campaign to deliberately disrupt plaintiffs' business . . . which was designed in part to interfere with and disrupt plaintiffs' relationships with their key at-will employees"—even though they "waited until after their resignations to offer jobs to plaintiffs' employees."[73]

One of the most publicized claims of raiding was the $100 million claim brought by retired partners, long time staff members and a trust benefiting certain retired partners and former partners and employees of Brobeck, Phlager & Harrison, LLP ("Brobeck") against Clifford Chance Rogers and Wells ("Clifford Chance") after the former chairman of Brobeck and 16 other partners left to join Clifford Chance.[74] Among other things, the plaintiffs alleged that the improper conduct consisted of solicitation of partners to move substantial numbers of Brobeck lawyers and clients to Clifford Chance[75] and the

---

[69]Gibbs v. Breed, Abbott & Morgan, 271 A.D.2d 180, 710 N.Y.S.2d 578 (1st Dep't 2000).

[70]Nixon Peabody LLP v. de Senilhes, Valsamdidis, Amsallem, Jonath, Flaicher Associes, 2008 WL 4256476 (NY Sup. Monroe 2008), citing A.L.I., Restatement (Third) of The Law Governing Lawyers § 9(3) (a), comment i and Joint Phila. And Pa. Bar Association Ethics Op. 99-100 (April 1999).

[71]*California:* Reeves v. Hanlon, 33 Cal.4th 1140, 17 Cal. Rptr.3d 289 95 P.3d 513 (2004).
　　Illinois: Dowd & Dowd, Ltd. v. Gleason, 352 Ill. App.3d 365, 287 Ill. Dec. 787, 816 N.E.2d 754 (2004).

[72]Dowd & Dowd, Ltd. v. Gleason, 352 Ill. App.3d 365, 287 Ill. Dec. 787, 816 N.E.2d 754 (2004).

[73]Reeves v. Hanlon, 33 Cal.4th 1140, 17 Cal. Rptr.3d 289, 95 P.3d 513 (2004).

[74]*See* Sandburg, "Records Reveal Financial Life of Brobeck Before Its Collapse." New York Law Journal, December 26, 2003, p. 16.

[75]Hanger v. Clifford Chance Rogers & Wells LLP, Case No. RG03120659, Complaint, Cal. Super. City of Alameda, ¶ 32, (Oct. 7, 2003). The case was later transferred to the bankruptcy court handling the Brobeck bankruptcy.

transfer to Clifford Chance of sensitive and proprietary data, including partner compensation, marketing materials, information about major matters and fees earned, and budgeting information.[76] They alleged that Clifford Chance was not only a "willing and knowledgeable participant" in these actions, but that it had "embarked upon a systematic campaign of predatory hiring of Brobeck personnel (including not only additional partners, but also associates and other employees) designed to further destabilize Brobeck, and misappropriate to itself Brobeck's good will and reputation."[77] These actions, according to the plaintiffs, were intended to and ultimately did cause Brobeck to default on its loans and cease operations in 2003.[78] In December 2004, the case was settled by a $5.5 million payment by Clifford Chance to the trustee of the Trust.

Ironically, Brobeck was on the opposite side of similar claims brought by partners of the former firm of Dickson, Carlson & Campillo ("DCC") after two of its partners joined Brobeck and took with them the firm's largest client, Baxter Healthcare Corporation (Baxter), a defendant in breast implant litigation nationwide.[79] In so doing, the departing partners provided Brobeck with detailed information concerning the profitability to DCC of the Baxter litigation, including DCC's historical billings per attorney, and met with Baxter to obtain its consent.[80]

DCC immediately dissolved and brought two actions against both Brobeck and the departing partners.[81] The first was for an accounting seeking to recover, among other things, part of the profits earned by defendants from the Baxter litigation.[82] The second sought damages for a variety of business torts.[83] The judge thereafter ruled that Brobeck's actions constituted unfair competition and directed an accounting. DCC was seeking restitution of the assets they lost to Brobeck, which it believed to be in the $10 million to $12 million range.[84] After eight years of litigation which cost both firms millions of

---

[76]*Id.*, at ¶ 20.

[77]*Id.*, at ¶ 28.

[78]*Id.*, at ¶ 34.

[79]Dickson, Carlson & Campillo v. Pole, 83 Cal. App.4th 436, 440, 99 Cal. Rptr.2d 678 (2000).

[80]*Id.*, 83 Cal. App.4th at 441.

[81]*Id.*

[82]*Id.*, 83 Cal. App.4th at 441-442.

[83]These claims encompassed (1) Brobeck's alleged offer to the departing partners "of substantial financial inducements to leave DCC and bring with them the book of business with Baxter," (2) the departing partners' "alleged act of turning over to Brobeck confidential DCC financial information" and (3) "Brobeck's alleged use of that confidential information in the preparation of a plan to induce Baxter to commit to transferring its business to Brobeck." *Id.*, 83 Cal. App.4th at 448, n.9.

[84]*Id.*

dollars, a jury found against Brobeck and one of the defecting partners and awarded the DCC partners $153,688.[85]

Another well publicized case is the currently pending nine-year old claim asserted by the now defunct firm of Ravin, Sarasohn, Cook, Baumgarten, Fisch & Rosen ("Ravin Sarasohn") against Lowenstein Sandler, P.C. ("Lowenstein") for its 2000 acquisition of virtually the entire bankruptcy group at Ravin Sarasohn. The acquisition included 15 lawyers (comprised of equity partners, non-equity partners and associates), as well as paralegal and support staff.[86] Within a month of the defections, Ravin Sarasohn collapsed and shortly thereafter sued Lowenstein and the three equity partners seeking compensatory and punitive damages, in an amount unspecified in the complaint, but which has been reported to amount to $42 million.[87]

The claim against Lowenstein was stayed, except for discovery, and for seven years the case proceeded in arbitration against the three equity partners pursuant to an arbitration provision in the Ravin Sarasohn equity shareholder's agreement.[88] After discovery was completed, Ravin Sarasohn voluntarily dismissed its claims against the individual defendants and the arbitration proceeded on the claim of one former equity partner as to his rights to severance payments under the equity shareholders' agreement.[89] In 2008, the arbitrator ruled that the former equity partner was entitled to his severance payments, but denied his request to share in any dissolution payments under that agreement, including any portion of the proceeds of the lawsuit against Lowenstein.[90]

---

[85]Sandburg, "Loss Not Too Pricey For Brobeck, Pole," The Legal Intelligencer, Vol. 228; No. 98; pg. 4 (May 21, 2003).

[86]Ravin, Sarasohn, Cook, Baumgarten, Fisch & Rosen, P.C. v. Lowenstein Sandler, P.C., Esx-L-6327-00 (Essex County Super. Ct., N.J.), Complaint; Law360, "NJ Case Could Test Limits Of 'Partner Poaching,'" February 3, 2009 (available at **http://www.law360.com/articles/85750**); Gottlieb, "Suit Over Firm's Collapse Tests Limits Of Poaching Lawyers," New Jersey Law Journal, February 3, 2009.

[87]Ravin, Sarasohn, Cook, Baumgarten, Fisch & Rosen, P.C. v. Lowenstein Sandler, P.C., Esx-L-6327-00 (Essex County Super. Ct., N.J.), Complaint; Law360, "NJ Case Could Test Limits Of 'Partner Poaching,'" February 3, 2009 (available at **http://www.law360.com/articles/85750**).

[88]Ravin, Sarasohn, Cook, Baumgarten, Fisch & Rosen, P.C. v. Lowenstein Sandler, P.C., Esx-L-6327-00 (Essex County Super. Ct., N.J.), Brief in Support of Defendant Lowenstein Sandler P.C.'s Motion For Partial Summary Judgment, January 5, 2009, pp. 8-9; Ravin, Sarasohn, Cook, Baumgarten, Fisch & Rosen, P.C. v. Lowenstein Sandler, P.C., Esx-L-6327-00 (Essex County Super. Ct., N.J.), Ravin Sarasohn's Brief in Opposition to Lowenstein Sandler's Motion for Partial Summary Judgment, pp. 2-3.

[89]Ravin, Sarasohn, Cook, Baumgarten, Fisch & Rosen, P.C. v. Lowenstein Sandler, P.C., Esx-L-6327-00 (Essex County Super. Ct., N.J.), Brief in Support of Defendant Lowenstein Sandler P.C.'s Motion For Partial Summary Judgment, January 5, 2009, p. 9.

[90]Ravin, Sarasohn, Cook, Baumgarten, Fisch & Rosen, P.C. v. Lowenstein Sandler, P.C., Esx-L-6327-00 (Essex County Super. Ct., N.J.), Ravin Sarasohn's Brief in Opposition to Lowenstein Sandler's Motion for Partial Summary Judgment, p. 11.

The case is, as of this time, proceeding against Lowenstein on claims of inducing breach of fiduciary duty, unfair competition, tortious interference with contractual relations, and tortious interference with prospective economic advantage.[91] Ravin Sarashon's allegations are that its former partners and Lowenstein executed a scheme to (i) "steal confidential Ravin Sarasohn financial information to enable it to secretly target and solicit key Ravin Sarasohn attorneys and personnel," (ii) "induce Ravin Sarasohn equity partners to break a 60 day notice of intent to withdraw provision contained in the firm's shareholder agreement," (iii) "pressure Ravin Sarasohn attorneys and staff to move to Lowenstein by creating an illusion that Ravin Sarasohn was a 'sinking ship,' " and (iv) "give notice of the defection only after Ravin Sarasohn attorneys and staff were fully committed to Lowenstein so that Ravin Sarasohn would have no ability to retain its employees or business."[92] Lowenstein disputes these claims and contends that Ravin Sarasohn's demise did not result from its acquisition, but rather from (i) previous significant losses of business and financial obligations after a name partner died and other major partners defected, (ii) high projected shortfalls in revenue, (iii) publicity regarding its financial condition and that it was being "shopped" to other firms, and (iv) the fact that many other attorneys were considering moves.[93] The case also presents an interesting question arising out of the bifurcated nature of the proceeding: Lowenstein has brought a motion for partial summary judgment claiming that Ravin Sarasohn's eleventh hour voluntary dismissal of its claims against its former equity partner with prejudice in the arbitration now collaterally estops it from bringing its claims against Lowenstein. The grounds asserted in support of this claim are that all of Lowenstein's claimed wrongful acts are based upon imputed liability for the acts that were alleged to have been taken by the former equity partner as Lowenstein's agent.[94] If the motion is denied, the case will proceed to trial.

Given that law firms—unlike other businesses—cannot enter into enforceable restraints to prevent competition or raiding, an approach which takes into account the impact of the departing partners' actions on the existing firm seems more consistent with the strong emphasis the courts have placed on the opportunity to compete. Indeed, to compensate for the unen-

---

[91]Ravin, Sarasohn, Cook, Baumgarten, Fisch & Rosen, P.C. v. Lowenstein Sandler, P.C., Esx-L-6327-00 (Essex County Super. Ct., N.J.), Reply Brief in Support of Defendant Lowenstein Sandler P.C.'s Motion For Partial Summary Judgment, January 5, 2009, p. 2.

[92]Ravin, Sarasohn, Cook, Baumgarten, Fisch & Rosen, P.C. v. Lowenstein Sandler, P.C., Esx-L-6327-00 (Essex County Super. Ct., N.J.), Ravin Sarasohn's Brief in Opposition to Lowenstein Sandler's Motion for Partial Summary Judgment, P. 1.

[93]Ravin, Sarasohn, Cook, Baumgarten, Fisch & Rosen, P.C. v. Lowenstein Sandler, P.C., Esx-L-6327-00 (Essex County Super. Ct., N.J.), Reply Brief in Support of Defendant Lowenstein Sandler P.C.'s Motion For Partial Summary Judgment, January 5, 2009, pp. 3-5.

[94]*Id.* at pp. 19, 23-25.

forceability of the restraints, imposing some limits on the partners' ability to secretly engineer a group departure is the only way a firm can have a fair opportunity to compete for the client and to give the client a realistic option to remain with the firm. One such approach would be to construe the fiduciary duty of partners as prohibiting partners from decimating a firm of an entire practice group at one time, or to afford the firm sufficient notice in such a situation to allow it to seek replacements if it so chooses. At a minimum, the intention with which such a move is undertaken should be considered in determining whether fiduciary obligations have been breached—irrespective of whether such conduct is accompanied by other improper conduct. A deliberate and surreptitious effort to destroy an entire practice area is hardly consonant with fiduciary obligations. This is particularly so where a firm has invested significant time and money in allowing the partners to develop that practice area.

On the other hand, the courts could develop a set of rules that better fit the reality of the ways in which the structure of law firms and the practice have changed. The body of partnership law that has developed over the years is premised, at its core, on the mutual economic risks partners assume.[95] It seeks to achieve a balance of rights and liabilities based on those risks by imposing fiduciary obligations of the highest order and permitting termination of the relationship at any time.[96] The weighty fiduciary duties central to a general partnership comprised only of equity partners is premised on the unlimited personal liability for other partners' acts. This rationale becomes less important as firms have been able to structure themselves in ways to limit personal liability, at least to some extent, through the use of LLPs, LLCs, and PCs. Accordingly, the entrenched notions that a partner should be able to leave at moment's notice may now have less force. Alternatively, the concept that the client always belongs to the firm may need to be reexamined, given the view of many lawyers, clients (and firms, at least when they are on the acquiring end) that clients hire a lawyer and not a firm and the ties that bind are more typically between the lawyer and the client. Thus, a rule could be adopted fitting this reality instead of one based on the axiom that it is the firm that is hired. In view of the facts that few courts have addressed the issue and several multimillion dollar judgments have been issued or settlements made, acquiring firms should be cautious about an acquisition that is so extensive or done in such a way that it effectively destroys or severely damages the ability of the other firm to compete.

Another issue that just beginning to be addressed in this context is the rights and obligations pertaining to contract or non-equity partners: Are they

---

[95]Wheeler v. Hurdman, 825 F.2d 257, 274-275, 276 (10th Cir. 1987), *cert. denied*, 484 U.S. 986 (1987).

[96]*Id.*

considered partners (and therefore allowed to be solicited by an equity partner before notifying one's partners) or employees?[97] This issue is of growing importance as firms are rapidly adding various levels of "partner" type positions.[98] Only one court, however, has directly addressed the issue.[99] The issue arose in a case involving claims asserted by a French law firm, Taylor Wessing France ("TWF"), that an American law firm, Nixon Peabody ("Nixon") had breached a nonsolicitation agreement entered into in connection with merger discussions, as well as aided and abetted TWF's founding partner in breaching his fiduciary duties to TWF.[100] When the merger discussions broke down, Nixon offered positions to the founding partner of TWF and 12 non-equity partners.[101] In addressing the aiding and abetting claim, the Court confronted the question as to whether the founding partner's conduct in recruiting the non-equity partners "prior to his giving notice to TWF of his planned departure, amounts to a breach of fiduciary duty."[102] The Court held that it was not.[103] As noted above, it first questioned whether the New York Appellate Court in *Gibbs*[104] really intended to draw "a clear distinction between partners and associates for purposes of the recruitment rule," but then held that even assuming that it did, the non-equity partners fell into the partner category for purposes of pre-resignation solicitation, at least where there were no aggravating circumstances, such as breaches of confidentiality or efforts to destroy the firm.[105] In reaching this conclusion, it focused primarily on the fact that "[w]hatever the precise functional differences the record discloses between partners and non-equity partners at TWF," "TWF held the non-equity partners

---

[97]The only other reported reference to the issue is in Pepe & Hazard v. Jones, 2002 Conn. Super. Lexis 2997 (Conn. Super. Sept. 11, 2002), in which the plaintiff law firm sought to introduce expert testimony which equated solicitation of contract partners with that of employees and staff. No reason for this categorization was provided. The Fall 2004 National Association of Legal Search Consultants Conference Report also advised to avoid pre-resignation solicitation of contract partners.

[98]This is true for a variety of reasons, not the least of which is the effort to make the status of contract partner meaningful.

[99]Nixon Peabody LLP v. de Senilhes, Valsamdidis, Amsallem, Jonath, Flaicher Associes, 2008 WL 4256476 (NY Sup. Monroe 2008).

[100]The non-solicitation clause provided that "neither firm would 'for two years from the date of this agreement . . . employ or offer partnership directly or indirectly . . . to any person who at the date of this agreement is a partner, a lawyer, or employee of . . . [the other firm.' "] *Id.* at 2.

[101]Under French law, the TWP lawyers remained at TWF for either a three to six month notice period. *Id.*

[102]*Id.* at 20.

[103]*Id.* at 24.

[104]Gibbs v. Breed, Abbott & Morgan, 271 A.D.2d 180, 710 N.Y.S.2d 578 (1st Dep't 2000).

[105]*Id.* at 20-24.

out to the public as partners of the firm" and concessions by TWF's counsel that the non-equity partners "have a certain status different from the employees, from the associates."[106] It buttressed its conclusion by finding that no aggravating circumstances existed because TWF had time to recover from the departures due to the three and six month notice periods required under French law, and there was no claim of an "incipit destruction of its entire business" or even its Paris office "by virtue of the departures."[107] In reaching this conclusion, the court focused solely on the public policies of lawyer mobility and client choice of counsel. It did not even mention the competing public policy concerns raised underlying fiduciary obligations to partners, much less make any effort to balance them.[108] Whether other courts will adopt this reasoning is an open question.

While in practice, contract partners often seek positions jointly with equity partners and thus are viewed by both the departing partners and the acquiring firm as governed by the mobility rules pertaining to partners, legally equating the two is questionable.

If the premise is accepted that partners have the right to withdraw from a partnership at any time and that the fiduciary obligations of partners to each other are deeply tied to the joint responsibility for both profits and losses—the *sine qua non* of partnership[109]—then the rationale for extending those rules to contract partners is not compelling. This is true even if a contract partner shares all of the other typical indicia of partnership (including participation in management). Absent the financial risk, the non-equity partner's stake in the enterprise is significantly different.[110] Even under limited liability structures, equity partners still have personal liability to the extent of a partner's capital contribution and his profit share and, thus, the mutual risks have not been eliminated.[111] Contract partners do not have assets at risk.

Moreover, given that the bundle of rights that contract partners have vary dramatically from full participation and voting rights (except perhaps for

---

[106]*Id.* at 23-24.

[107]*Id.*

[108]See, Krauss, "Validity of Nonsolicitation Pacts Among Lawyers Shrinks," New York Law Journal, October 21, 2008, p. 4, col. 4 for an analysis of the ruling.

[109]Graham v. Commissioner, 8 B.T.A. 1081, 1088 (Bd. Tax App. 1927) (dissenting opinion) ("one of the factors almost universally recognized as a sine qua non of the partnership relation, to wit, a sharing, as a principal, of the profits and losses of the business."). *See also,* Missan v. Schoenfeld, 95 A.D.2d 198, 465 N.Y.S.2d 706 (1st Dep't 1983).

[110]The fact that the firm holds the person out to the world as a partner should not impact on this determination, since typically any contract partner would seek indemnification from the equity partners for any liability that would be imposed on that account.

[111]*See, e.g.,* N.Y. Partnership Law § 105.

making partners) to merely an honorific or glorified associate, a principled rule pertaining to all contract partners is difficult to apply. This is evident in the struggle the courts have been having with this issue in the employment context.[112] Accordingly, departing partners and acquiring firms desiring to err on the side of caution in the dearth of precedent may well choose to apply the employee rules to contract partners.

---

[112]*See, e.g.*, Clackamas Gastroenterology Associates, P. C. v. Wells 538 U.S. 440, 123 S.Ct. 1673 (U.S., 2003).

The Law Pertaining to Notice V

In planning for a departure or an acquisition, it is important to anticipate when the move will actually occur. While ideally the acquiring firm and the lateral partner or group would like to pick the date, obligations regarding notice that the departing partner may have to his existing firm or the firm's reaction to notice of the departure may well impact on the decision.

A partner generally has no duty to disclose that he is considering withdrawing from a firm, but there are circumstances where such a duty may arise. One circumstance is when the partner is aware that the existing firm is considering undertaking an obligation in reliance on or with the reasonable expectation that the partner will continue to be a member of the firm.[113] Such obligations could include moving to new offices,[114] taking on additional space, hiring staff,[115] or making capital

---

[113]Graubard Mollen Dannet & Horowitz v. Moskovitz 86 N.Y.2d 112, 629 N.Y.S.2d. 1009, 1011, 653 N.E.2d 1179 (1995). Obviously, this obligation depends on how significant the partner or the business he controls is to the firm and what the firm is planning on doing.

[114]Graubard Mollen Dannet & Horowitz v. Moskovitz 86 N.Y.2d 112, 629 N.Y.S.2d. 1009, 1011, 653 N.E.2d 1179 (1995) (firm contended it would not have taken on a $1.5 million dollar lease for new space if it had known that the defendants were leaving).

[115]Hillman, "Loyalty in the Firm: A Statement of General Principles on the Duties of Partners Withdrawing from Law Firms," 55 Wash. & Lee L. Rev. 997, 1007 (1998).

expenditures.[116] In addition, disclosure issues are implicated to the extent profits or bonuses are (or the firm may later claim to be) allocated based not only on past performance, but with expectations of future performance.[117]

A second circumstance in which disclosure may be required is if other partners, in good faith, make inquiries as to a partner's plans regarding withdrawal. While a partner does not have to volunteer his plans, he cannot lie to his partners.[118]

Once an offer is accepted, a partner has a duty to disclose his intended departure promptly.[119] A failure to do so could be viewed as deception and expose both the partner and the acquiring firm to a claim of damages for breach of fiduciary duty or aiding and abetting breach of fiduciary duty, respectively, if the prior firm can demonstrate that it incurred damage as a result of the delayed notice.[120]

The acquiring firm should also be aware of any contractual notice requirements the departing partner may be subject to—which most typically range from 30 to 60 days but can extend to six months or longer. There is, however, a serious question as to the enforceability of such notice provisions. The New Jersey Supreme Court, the highest state court to have opined on the matter, cautioned that while it would not hold such provisions *per se* unenforceable, "firms must guard against provisions that unreasonably delay an attorney's orderly transition from one firm to another."[121] The court directed the State Bar Committee to study the issue.[122] This matter may soon

---

[116]*Id.*, 55 Wash. & Lee L. Rev. at 1015 (1998). *See also*, Corwin, "Response to Loyalty in the Firm: A Statement of General Principles on the Duties of Partners Withdrawing from Law Firms" 55 Wash. & Lee L. Rev. 1055, 1065 (1998).

[117]In Dowd & Dowd, Ltd. v. Gleason, 352 Ill. App.3d 365, 287 Ill. Dec. 787, 816 N.E.2d 754, 797, 799 (2004), the court held that the departing partners had breached their fiduciary duties to the firm by paying down the firm's bank line of credit "without authorization, in order to present a better financial statement for themselves when obtaining a line of credit" for the new firm they were forming, "voting and accepting large bonuses for themselves and their friends and family without disclosure that they would be leaving" and "strip[ing] [the firm] of cash reserves."

[118]Graubard Mollen Dannet & Horowitz v. Moskovitz, 86 N.Y.2d 112, 629 N.Y.S.2d 1009, 1011, 653 N.E.2d 1179 (1995) ("lying to partners about plans to leave . . . would not be consistent with a partner's fiduciary duties."). See also, Hillman, "Loyalty in the Firm: A Statement of General Principles on the Duties of Partners Withdrawing from Law Firms," 55 Wash. & Lee L. Rev. 997, 1008 (1998).

[119]Hillman, "Loyalty in the Firm: A Statement of General Principles on the Duties of Partners Withdrawing from Law Firms," 55 Wash. & Lee L. Rev. 997, 1006 (1998).

[120]*Id.*

[121]Borteck v. Riker, Danzig, Scherer, Hyland & Perretti, 179 N.J. 246, 844 A.2d 521, 531 (2004).

[122]*Id.*, 844 A.2d at 522. In response to the court's request, on March 3, 2006, the Professional Responsibility Rules Committee submitted its report, stating as follows:

In Borteck v. Riker, 179 N.J. 246 (2004), the Supreme Court . . . directed the PRRC to consider whether an express rule or more explicit guidance is needed in re-be revisited as a pending New Jersey case raises the issue as to whether an acquiring firm engaged in wrongful conduct by allegedly inducing the partners it was acquiring to breach a 60-day notice withdrawal provision in their existing partnership agreement.[123] Factors that a court may consider as to the reasonableness of a notice provision include (1) whether there is any legitimate reason for the delay (such as a true need for the departing partner's services to transition matters at the former firm), (2) the past practice of the firm when partners have sought to withdraw, and (3) the possibility of retribution or acrimony that could affect the departing partners or client matters if they stayed in the firm for the notice period.[124] Irrespective of whether the notice provisions are enforceable, however, the acquiring firm should take care not to impose any conditions that could be deemed to interfere with the departing partner's ability to comply with those obligations.

In view of the fact that the departing partner, even after notification, may not solicit clients using the existing firm's resources or on its time, solicitation efforts will necessarily be more circumscribed. Thus, it is in the departing partner's and the acquiring firm's interest for the incoming lateral partner to seek a waiver of any notice requirements and/or accomplish whatever is needed to make an orderly transition as soon as possible.

---

spect of a partnership agreement's notice departure provisions. As regards notice-departure provisions, the PRRC is of the view that the enforceability of such provisions will need to be determined under the circumstances of the specific contractual agreement and on a case-by-case analysis. The PRRC is of the view that explicit guidance in rule form is not helpful for contractual notice-departure provisions.

[123]See, Ravin, Sarasohn, Cook, Baumgarten, Fisch & Rosen, P.C. v. Lowenstein Sandler, P.C., Esx-L-6327-00 (Essex County Super. Ct., N.J.), Complaint.

[124]Hillman, "Loyalty in the Firm: A Statement of General Principles on the Duties of Partners Withdrawing from Law Firms," 55 Wash. & Lee L. Rev. 997, 1004-1005 (1998).

The Law Pertaining to Due Diligence

Following the rules of client and employee solicitation can protect the acquiring firm from a lawsuit from the existing firm, but only due diligence can protect the firm from taking on a lateral who is more likely to be a liability than an asset. Due diligence should cover five areas:

(1) professional history;
(2) personal history;
(3) anticipated portable business;
(4) conflicts; and
(5) obligations to the prior firm.

Four of these categories raise minimal legal issues. Due diligence with respect to portable business—perhaps the most important issue to the acquiring firm—is a minefield.

A. Professional Due Diligence

The purpose of professional due diligence is for the acquiring firm to assure itself that the potential lateral has the appropriate credentials, is competent, ethical, and has not caused problems at prior firms. A thorough investigation of a potential lateral's professional history would examine the following issues:

- ◆ Verifying the lateral's credentials and prior work history
- ◆ Confirming the lateral's competence and work quality

◆ Determining a litigation lateral's win/loss record

◆ Investigating whether the lateral was disciplined at prior firms

◆ Investigating whether the lateral was sanctioned by a court, subject to disciplinary action, or refused admission to practice

◆ Investigating whether there are any previous, ongoing, or potential malpractice claims against the lateral

◆ Determining whether there are any previous, ongoing, or potential investigations with respect to the lateral

◆ Ascertaining the lateral's professional reputation

◆ Obtaining professional references from partners in the acquiring firm, other lawyers, clients, former partners or employers, and adversaries.

While investigation of some of these issues may present practical or timing issues, there would generally be no legal obstacles or liabilities related to obtaining this information. Perhaps the most difficult information to obtain from outside sources would be any problems experienced at prior firms. Generally, a prior firm is under no duty to disclose negative information, although in some states claims for negligent misrepresentation are emerging where a former employer knows that the former employee engaged in conduct that the prior firm reasonably believes would pose a danger to others.[125] On the other hand, if the prior firm reveals negative information, which the lateral believes is untrue or defamatory, it may end up being sued by the lateral.[126] On balance, the prior firm probably has more to fear from reporting negative history than in not reporting it. There is, of course, no prohibition against asking the potential lateral partner these questions directly. Any misrepresentations would then be a basis for future actions, if necessary.

B. Personal Due Diligence

Personal due diligence is designed to uncover anything about the potential lateral partner's personal background that could create a problem for the acquiring firm. The key areas of concern are (1) whether there have been any civil or criminal claims that would be problematic from either a legal or public relations standpoint, (2) whether there are any serious personal or finan-

---

[125]Sperber, "When Nondisclosure Becomes Misrepresentation: Shaping Employer Liability for Incomplete Job References," 32 U.S.F. L. Rev. 405 (1998).

[126]*Cf.*, Jensen v. Pillsbury Winthrop,CV-02-0191966-S, (Conn. Super. 2002), Complaint, filed in Connecticut Superior Court, Stamford-Norwalk District, October 14, 2002 available at **http://www.americanlawyer.com/pdf/101402jensen-complaint.pdf**; Pitcock v. Kasowitz, Benson, Torres & Friedman, LLP 08 Civ. 5166 SDNY; complaint available at **http://amlaw daily.typepad.com/amlawdaily/files/jeremy_pitcock_pitcock_v.%20Kasowitz_FINAL%20 Complaint%20(pdf)-0001.PDF**.

cial issues of the sort that may raise the risk of disciplinary or ethical violations, and (3) whether there is any involvement in other business activities. To this end, the following areas should be explored:

- Determining whether there are any previous, ongoing, or potential civil claims or criminal charges against the lateral
- Determining whether there are any previous, ongoing, or potential civil judgments; or criminal convictions against the lateral
- Determining whether the lateral has declared bankruptcy or is experiencing financial problems
- Determining whether the lateral is in the midst of a divorce
- Determining whether the lateral is involved in other business ventures, entrepreneurial activities, boards or directorships
- Determining whether the lateral is in good health
- Determining whether the lateral has had a history of alcoholism or drug abuse
- Obtaining personal references.

When these inquiries are being made about a potential equity partner, there are generally no legal obstacles or liabilities related to obtaining this information. If the potential lateral is being considered as a contract partner, counsel or employee, some of these questions could be problematic under the various federal, state, and local employment laws.

C. Portable Business and Practice Due Diligence

From the acquiring firm's point of view, the driving factor for the acquisition of a lateral partner, as well as the basis for proposed compensation, is the anticipation that the potential lateral partner can bring in significant business. Accordingly, portable business due diligence is the effort to ascertain that the projections of the potential lateral partner are accurate and not merely "puffing." Unlike the issues of professional and personal due diligence, vetting business opportunities raises numerous issues involving fiduciary duties and confidential information. Ideally, the areas of inquiry would include:

- Presentation of a business plan by the potential lateral partner
- Determining the lateral's expectations with respect to portable clients and the reasonableness of those expectations, including the nature of the clients, the likely quantity of work and the quality of the work
- Identifying previous major matters or deals
- Investigating the growth potential of the anticipated client base and practice area

- ◆ Determining the extent and depth of the lateral's relationship with anticipated clients through the following questions:
  —Is the potential lateral the main contact person with the clients?
  —Are there others remaining at the firm with significant ties to the clients?
  —Do remaining partners at the firm have the ability to continue to do the work?
  —How much work does the lateral perform personally?
  —What will be the likely reaction of the present firm and success of their efforts to keep the clients?
  —Would the client likely have any issues with the acquiring firm?
- ◆ Ascertaining the anticipated needs to service clients through the following questions:
  —How many attorneys, paralegals, or other staff will be required and at what experience level?
  —What is the anticipated cost of staffing needs?
  —Are there any other requirements of any clients or the practice area that require a financial commitment, such as political and/or charitable contributions, conference attendance, or special materials or personnel?
- ◆ Determining whether there are opportunities for cross-selling
- ◆ Determining the needs for office and conference room space
- ◆ Determining whether there will be any requirements to advance costs in any significant amounts in connection with the practice
- ◆ Determining whether there are any insurance needs or issues
- ◆ Determining likely billing rates
- ◆ Determining likely hours to be billed
- ◆ Determining whether contingency work is involved
- ◆ Determining likely collection issues, including the timing and amount of anticipated payments and write-offs.

Much of the information needed to fully answer these questions is clearly information which the existing firm—as well as a court—would likely view as confidential. Accordingly, the acquiring firm faces challenges in obtaining assurances without exposing itself or the potential lateral partner to claims involving the improper dissemination or use of confidential information.

In recognition of the reality that the acquiring firm is going to require some verification of the potential lateral partner's claims regarding both historical and anticipated business generation to make an offer, the rules as to what possibly confidential information can be furnished appear to be bending. Once again, an attempt is being made to strike a balance between (1) the interest of the firm which the attorney is leaving in protecting non-public information and its right to be free of competition from its partners, and (2) the attorney's right to move and the client's right of choice.

While there is some case law with respect to the disclosure of client identities and client lists,[127] there is far less guidance on other types of information. Generally, the tests the courts use in determining whether information is confidential is whether (1) the information is publicly available or known outside the business, (2) the information is able to be duplicated and what resources have been expended in developing it, and (3) and to what extent the firm has taken measures to protect the information.[128]

The identity of individual firm clients generally is not considered confidential information.[129] Indeed, often the fact that the firm represents a client has been publicized (such as through announcements of transactions in legal media or listing on a firm's web site) or publicly available through court or other public records.[130] The lack of confidentiality is also evident from the general rule that identification of any particular client is not considered privileged.[131] For purposes of lateral movement, the line with respect to client identification is drawn between clients with whom the potential lateral had a direct and personal relationship and those which he did not.[132] Thus, courts have generally held that lawyers are permitted to disclose the clients

---

[127]*See, e.g.*, Willis v. Superior Court, 112 Cal. App.3d 277, 291, 169 Cal. Rptr. 301 (1980).

[128]*See, e.g.*:

> *Connecticut:* Early, Ludwick & Sweeney, LLC v. John-Henry Steele,1998 Conn. Super. (1998). LEXIS 2256 (Conn. Super. Aug. 6, 1998).
> *Ohio:* Fred Siegel Co., L.P.A. v. Arter & Hadden, 1999 Ohio 260, 85 Ohio St.3d 171, 707 N.E.2d 853 (1999).

[129]*See, e.g.*, Willis v. Superior Court, 112 Cal. App.3d 277, 291, 169 Cal. Rptr. 301 (1980) ("It is the majority American rule that the identity and address of an attorney's client is not per se a confidential communication protected by the attorney client privilege. . ."). *But see* Liew v. Breen, 640 F.2d 1046, 1049 (9th Cir. 1981), noting that state and federal courts have recognized a limited exception to the general rule where the disclosure of the client's identity would uncover client confidences.

[130]*See, e.g.*, **www.searchsystems.net**; The PACER (Public Access to Court Electronic Records) system.

[131]*See* Willis v. Superior Court, 112 Cal. App.3d 277, 291, 169 Cal. Rptr. 301 (1980).

[132]*Connecticut:* Early, Ludwick & Sweeney, LLC v. John-Henry Steele,1998 Conn. Super. (1998). LEXIS 2256 (Conn. Super. Aug. 6, 1998).
New York: Gibbs v. Breed, Abbott & Morgan, 271 A.D.2d 180, 710 N.Y.S.2d 578, 582-583 (1st Dep't 2000). *See also,* Graubard Mollen Dannet & Horowitz v. Moskovitz, 86 N.Y.2d 112, 629 N.Y.S.2d. 1009, 1010, 653 N.E.2d 1179 (1995).
Ohio: Fred Siegel Co., L.P.A. v. Arter & Hadden, 1999 Ohio 260, 85 Ohio St.3d 171, 707 N.E.2d 853, 859 (Ohio 1999).

they worked with personally, as well as to take the names and contact information for clients which whom they worked with personally once they leave.[133] On the other hand, client lists encompassing the firm's clients as a whole have been held to be confidential and even protectable as trade secrets.[134]

As to information regarding the details of the representation of the clients and the business or operations of the firm, there is limited case law addressing specific types of information.[135] Recommendations as to what is permissible vary widely. At one end of the spectrum, it has been suggested that, to the greatest extent possible, the vetting firm look for and use data available from public sources and accept non-public financial information only about the candidate and from the candidate.[136] Under this view, non-public information, such as historical billings, collections, realizations, billing rates, and future generation generally should not be broken down by client, but should be gross numbers for all clients.[137] One well respected commenta-

---

[133]*See, e.g.:*

> *Connecticut:* Early, Ludwick & Sweeney, LLC v. John-Henry Steele,1998 Conn. Super. (1998). LEXIS 2256 (Conn. Super. Aug. 6, 1998) (departing lawyer permitted to take a list of sixteen clients he had represented in pediatric lead poisoning cases while at firm containing names).
> *New York:* Gibbs v. Breed, Abbott & Morgan, 271 A.D.2d 180, 710 N.Y.S.2d 578, 582-583 (1st Dep't 2000) (departing lawyers may take rolodexes).
> *Ohio:* Fred Siegel Co., L.P.A. v. Arter & Hadden, 1999 Ohio 260, 85 Ohio St.3d 171, 707 N.E.2d 853, 859 (Ohio 1999) (associate could take rolodex containing names and contacts of clients she worked with).

[134]*See, e.g.:*

> *California:* Reeves v. Hanlon, 33 Cal.4th 1140, 17 Cal. Rptr.3d 289, 95 P.3d 513 (2004) (law firm client list deemed to be a trade secret which were misappropriated by withdrawing partners where firm took measures to protect it, firm was engaged in specialized area of practice, and list was developed over twenty-one years based on advertising, client intake, representation and good will).
> *Ohio:* Fred Siegel Co., L.P.A. v. Arter & Hadden, 1999 Ohio 260, 85 Ohio St.3d 171, 707 N.E.2d 853, 859 (Ohio 1999) (where associate took sixty three page list including names, addresses and phone numbers of hundreds of clients; court held it was an issue of material fact as to whether firm took steps to protect its list).

[135]Early, Ludwick & Sweeney, LLC v. John-Henry Steele, CV 980409063S, 1998 Conn. Super. LEXIS 2256 (Conn. Super. Aug. 6, 1998), (departing lawyer took list of sixteen clients he had represented in pediatric lead poisoning cases while at firm containing names, addresses, telephone numbers, guardians, blood lead levels and insurance coverage; information held not to be confidential since lawyer had worked the cases, established relationships with clients, and was entitled to notify them of change in employment so they could continue to work with him; in addition there was no effort on part of firm to safeguard the secrecy of information).

[136]Fall 2004 National Association of Legal Search Consultants Conference Report.

[137]*Id.*

tor distinguishes between "non-public firm-specific information," i.e., "information pertaining to the finances, practice, and operations of a firm," and "client-specific information."[138] His recommendation is that limited items of confidential firm information and client-specific information may be disclosed by a partner to another firm in connection with that partner's exploration of possible affiliation with the firm. The firm information that may be disclosed is "the minimum necessary to allow a general assessment of the nature of the partner's practice, the resources required to support the practice, potential conflicts with existing clients of the firm, and an appropriate range of compensation."[139] Client-specific information may be disclosed if the (1) potential lateral partner reasonably believes the client is likely to follow him to a new firm and would not object to the disclosure, (2) information relates directly to the legal services provided by the firm to the client, and (3) client could disclose it to another firm.[140] One possible justification for a rule could derive from an analogy to privilege. It is up to the client, not to the firm, to decide whether to waive any privilege. Thus, if the client could disclose the information and would not object to the lawyer disclosing it, the prior firm has no basis to do so.

With respect to disclosing specific information about associates or staff, the acquiring firm should not ask for or accept the names, salaries, and billing rates of those employees the potential lateral partner would hope to bring.[141] Rather, staffing needs should be addressed generally, by the number and level of experience of associates, paralegals, or other staff that may be needed.[142]

As a result, the acquiring firm should seek the minimum amount of information necessary to allow it to generally assess the nature of the practice, the number and seniority or both of the professional and non-professional staff required to service the practice, and the overall likely profitability of the practice. The one rule that the acquiring firm should rigidly follow, however, is not to ask for or accept any financial documentation or analyses which are computer generated or otherwise internally produced by the lateral's present firm, redacted or otherwise. In addition, to avoid any claim that premature

---

[138]Hillman, "Loyalty in the Firm: A Statement of General Principles on the Duties of Partners Withdrawing from Law Firms," 55 Wash. & Lee L. Rev. 997, 1019 (1998).

[139]*Id.*, 55 Wash. & Lee L. Rev. at 1023.

[140]*Id.* This article also suggests that client consent is a necessary condition either before or after the fact. This seems to be a problematic requirement as prior consent cannot be obtained based on the pre-resignation non-solicitation rule and after the fact consent provides no protection at the time of the disclosure.

[141]Gibbs v. Breed, Abbott & Morgan, 271 A.D.2d 180, 710 N.Y.S.2d 578 (1st Dep't 2000).

[142]*Id.*

solicitation occurred, the acquiring firm should not ask for or accept any specific client contact information or individual specific staffing information before the transition.

D. Conflicts Due Diligence

To be able to assess any conflict of interest issues, the acquiring firm should focus on two points: (1) are there existing conflicts, and (2) are there likely to be conflicts in the future?

To determine whether there are existing conflicts, the acquiring firm should determine whether any of the potential clients have been adverse to present or former clients of the acquiring firm, and if so, in what matters. Inquiry should also be made as to the clients the lateral personally worked with, even if it is not anticipated that those clients will follow, as disqualification and conflict issues could still result.

It is also important for the acquiring firm and the potential lateral partner to ascertain whether the client bases are compatible. One avenue of inquiry is whether the lateral's clients are likely to be adverse to the acquiring firm's existing clients or categories of clients. Incompatible categories include such groups as management vs. labor, institutional clients vs. customers, plaintiff orientation vs. defendant orientation, or insurers vs. insured. Another avenue of inquiry is whether the lateral's clients are or are likely to be objectionable or distasteful to the acquiring firm's existing clients or partners. This could occur if, for example, a lateral represents a major competitor to an existing client and the existing client does not want its law firm to represent any competitors or if the lateral's client interest with respect to particular issues would be adverse to those of an existing client. Another area of incompatibility may involve client or partner objection for what may be termed political issues, such as representation of certain countries or companies that may engage in practices, make products, or take positions on issues with which the firm may not want to be associated.

Generally it is not a problem to disclose names of clients for conflicts purposes. However, no client of either the potential lateral partner or the acquiring firm should be contacted or consulted about any conflicts that may be discovered before notice is given to the departing partner's existing firm. Screening and analysis of any potential conflict should only be done internally. If the potential conflicts are serious or for some reason cannot be fully vetted, the offer of lateral partnership needs to be made contingent on determining and clearing conflicts. Moreover, it is important to do this screening as soon as possible inasmuch as firewalls or other devices that could be used to avoid disqualification may need to be erected as soon as the lateral arrives.

E. Due Diligence Regarding Obligations to the Prior Firm

While restrictions that provide disincentives for leaving are generally unenforceable,[143] there are certain situations where the existing firm may have some continuing claim with respect to transferred work. The main circumstance under which this would arise is in contingency cases. The existing firm has two interests: (1) it may be entitled to a portion of any subsequent settlement, and (2) it may be entitled to be paid any disbursements it expended before the file is transferred. In contingent fee cases, contractual fee arrangements and departure provisions regarding those fees may be enforceable if they are reasonable.[144] Accordingly, the acquiring firm should inquire into whether there are any such agreements, as well as investigate what the existing firm may be entitled to on a *quantum meruit* basis.

The acquiring firm should also determine whether the clients are likely to incur any loss or expense if they choose to follow the departing partner. For example, while it is very rare, at least one court has enforced a limited penalty on account of an early discharge as the condition of having had the benefit of a reduced fee.[145] This may well impact whether the client will likely follow the lateral, or whether it might require economic concessions to do so.

F. Methods of Due Diligence

One of the key factors in doing due diligence is being aware that whatever documentation the acquiring firm seeks or creates will be discoverable in any lawsuit that may result between the existing firm and the new lateral partner and/or the acquiring firm. The acquiring firm should therefore be careful that what it seeks and what it accepts is in conformity with the rules set out herein.

The key methods of obtaining personal, professional, portable business, and other due diligence include all or some combination of the following: (1) questionnaires, (2) documents, (3) background checks, (4) interviews, and (5) reference checks.

---

[143]*See* Section II, *supra*.

[144]*See, e.g.*, Groen, Laveson, Goldberg, Rubenstone v. Kancher, 362 N.J.Super. 350, 827 A.2d 1163 (2003) (attorney was obligated to remit percentage of contingency fee received to prior firm because the firm was entitled to compensation for the services provided prior to attorney's departure).; Appleton v. Bondurant & Appleton, P.C., 68 Va. Cir. 208, 2005 WL 3579087 *19 (Va. Cir. Ct. 2005) (claims of quantum meruit asserted by remaining attorney for work in cases that left with departing lawyers for work done in cases left behind.)

[145]Cohen v. Radio-Electronics Officers Union, Dist. 3, NMEBA, 146 N.J. 140, 679 A.2d 1188 (N.J. 1996).

1. Questionnaires

Due diligence should begin with a comprehensive questionnaire. The questionnaire, which can be tailored to the acquiring firm, should seek as much appropriate information as possible, while at the same time serve as a guide to the potential lateral as to what information should not be supplied. The questionnaire can then be used as a springboard for further due diligence with respect to the information provided.

The questionnaire should be one of the first steps in the acquisition process. As such, it is a good vehicle to communicate, in writing, what is and is not permissible for the lateral to do during the process. In particular, the questionnaire should advise the incoming partner that (1) the acquiring firm is not asking for and does not want him to provide any confidential information, and (2) the lateral partner should not engage in any solicitation of clients or employees of the existing firm in connection with the interviewing process. The questionnaire is an excellent means to obtain the information identified under the personal and professional due diligence headings. With respect to the business and practice due diligence questions, the questionnaire should only seek general information with a focus on what is anticipated in terms of business, billings, collections, time commitments and practice needs, as opposed to any detailed historical information or specifics about individual clients, practices or billing rates of the existing firm or its employees. To avoid conflicts, the acquiring firm should obtain the names of current and former clients for prior three years.

2. Documents

The acquiring firm should ask the lateral being interviewed to provide his or her resume, personal financial statements and/or tax returns (with access to these limited to one or two members of the acquiring firm), a pro forma business plan, and certificates of good standing. As previously noted, the acquiring firm should not ask for any financial documentation or analyses which are computer generated or otherwise internally produced by the lateral's present firm, redacted or otherwise. Nor should it ask for or generate any internal documents that even suggest that it sought any assurances that business would be transferred or obtained any such assurances.

3. Background Checks

Background checks can be informal or formal. Informal checks are those that can be done without hiring an investigative agency. In particular, there is an enormous amount of information that can be obtained about an individual lawyer and clients through Internet searches. Lexis or Westlaw searches should reveal cases in which the lateral was counsel or a party or legal articles he published. Nexis or search engine searches may reveal transactions the lateral was involved in and articles about him or events he was involved in (both legal and non-legal). Licensing can be verified through bar- and court-sponsored cites. Sanctions and disciplinary actions are also available on government-, bar- and court-sponsored cites. Inquiries should certainly be made of all of the members of the acquiring firm to see if they have had any personal contacts with the specific lateral and judicious use can be made of personal contacts.

Formal background checks can also be employed. These are often expensive and intrusive, but may be called for in certain situations. It is a good idea to advise the potential lateral if such searches are to be done and to obtain written permission to do them. If permission is not forthcoming, that in and of itself can be a red flag. The kinds of searches that can be performed include:

- Education and licensing credentials
- Employment history
- Civil and criminal court filings
- Lien searches
- Bankruptcy filings
- Divorce filings
- Credit check
- Third-party reference check
- Psychological evaluations
- Health evaluations

4. Interviewing Process

Lawyers are trained to ask questions and evaluate answers. Lawyers at the acquiring firm should use those skills in interviewing laterals to obtain information and evaluate the lateral, much as they would during a client intake. All too often the interview process turns more into an effort by the members of the acquiring firm to try and describe the firm and to convince the lateral that he should come there, instead of taking the opportunity to really question and find out about the lateral. This can happen for a variety of reasons, ranging from an eagerness to acquire the lateral based on minimal information, a reluctance to take time away from billable work to spend substantial time with the candidate, and the lack of any clear agenda for the interview. What then results are general questions, hearsay and general representations regarding portable business and projected synergies.

As in any interview, more information is learned by listening than talking. It is important to find out why the lateral is looking to leave his or her current firm and what he or she hopes will be different. Work history and any gaps between positions need to be examined. This information should be elicited before the potential partner is told what the acquiring firm is looking for so that answers are not tailored to what the lateral thinks the interviewer wants to hear. The interviewers should listen critically, as they would to a client, and if there is some part of the story that does not make sense, ask questions about it. Interviews with different partners or groups of partners may be devoted to specific areas or have specific goals. Subjects that can be covered well through interviewing are interpersonal skills, marketing skills, cultural expectations, technical competence, and questions regarding the lateral's practice.

5. Reference Checks

Reference checks, while a means of due diligence, have limited usefulness. First, there are timing issues. The most significant reference check—with the clients—generally may not be done until after the offer is extended and the hired attorney notifies his current firm that he is leaving. By that time, checking a reference with a client makes little business sense. If the lateral has the relationship with the client he claims, he or she will be able to introduce it to the firm and the discussion will be focused on marketing the firm to the client. If he does not have that relationship, it is too late to be a factor as to whether to make an offer. There is also obviously a timing issue with respect to obtaining a reference from the existing firm. Moreover, the likelihood of finding out anything negative from the existing firm is minimal. For one thing, if the firm has asked the partner to leave or is happy to see that partner gone, it is unlikely to discourage the offer because a problem will then be taken off its hands. Ironically, this is particularly true if there are the kind of problems that the acquiring firm might most like to hear about—such as sexual harassment claims, malpractice claims, or bad citizenship issues. In addition, the references that a potential hire provides that may be contacted before he or she is actually hired are hand picked and likely to give glowing appraisals.

The only references which are going to be useful are likely to be former partners of the lateral at his or her current firm who have since left the firm, former partners of the lateral at a former firm, or people in the acquiring firm itself who may have worked with the potential lateral or know someone who has (and the lateral has no objection to that person being contacted).

G. Due Diligence with Respect to Non-Partners

It is important to note that many of the questions or issues addressed with respect to partners would be improper under the federal, state, and local employment laws for the firm to raise with potential employees in the group the partner may desire to bring with him. Here, the firm is limited to the same kind of due diligence that would be done with any employee hire.

The Law Pertaining to Files VII

Other than the general obligation not to take any privileged or confidential documents (from either the client's or the firm's perspective), there is little law as to what a lawyer can or cannot take, particularly in the area of electronic files. A New York appellate court held that an attorney's client list is not confidential, nor are the lawyers' desk copies of correspondence written to the client, at least where such documents are typically taken, the firm has a copy, and there is no contractual obligation against doing so.[146] It is also the general practice that partners can take with them their own personal copies of documents or forms they drafted, again provided that there is no agreement not to do so and the documents do not contain confidential client information.[147] Whatever is appropriate to take in hard copy is likely to be

---

[146]Gibbs v. Breed, Abbott & Morgan, 271 A.D.2d 180, 710 N.Y.S.2d 578 (1st Dep't 2000). In so ruling, the court rejected the firm's claim the taking of desk copies of correspondence should not be excused by that the fact that duplicate copies of the correspondence were contained somewhere in the firm's thousands of the files because the desk files were the easiest way of knowing which of those files had any current activity. This claim had been upheld by the trial court. 181 Misc.2d at 349. Though the court did not mention it in rejecting this argument, there are other ways to determine matters on which there was current activity, such as time sheets. The court also did not address the possibility that the information contained in letters could well contain privileged matter which a firm has a definite interest in assuring does not leave the firm.

[147]Hillman, "Loyalty in the Firm: A Statement of General Principles on the Duties of Partners Withdrawing From Law Firms" 55 Wash. & Lee L. Rev. 997, 1025 (1998). See also Gibbs v. Breed, Abbott & Morgan, 271 A.D.2d 180, 710 N.Y.S.2d 578 (1st Dep't 2000).

permissible to take as an electronic file. On the other hand, it would be improper for the departing partner to download the firm's entire bank of forms in his department or practice area.

These rules may change if there are contractual agreements that provide otherwise.[148] For example, if a partner signs a partnership agreement in which he agrees that he will not remove any forms or documents from the firm—irrespective of whether he created them or the firm had duplicate copies—that provision may be enforceable. The best argument against the enforceability of such a provision would be that such a prohibition improperly inhibits an attorney's ability to move or his ability to represent a client.[149] Unlike businesses or even other professions, the tools of a lawyer's trade are often the forms and documents he creates. Indeed, the prior firm may well have had the benefit of forms or documents that the partner brought with him from a prior firm. Moreover, to the extent that the documents may be publicly filed, there is little justification for a firm to prevent the lawyer from taking a copy other than to make it more difficult to compete and service clients. That, however, flies directly in the face of the strong public policies of attorney mobility and the ability to efficiently service clients.

Client files cannot be taken absent a written authorization from the client directing the lateral's former firm to release them.[150] Such releases may also be subject to any retaining lien the former firm may have.[151]

---

[148]Gibbs v. Breed, Abbott & Morgan, 271 A.D.2d 180, 710 N.Y.S.2d 578 (1st Dep't 2000).

[149]*See* Hillman, "The Property Wars of Law Firms: Of Client Lists, Trade Secrets and the Fiduciary Duties of Law Partners," 30 Fla. St. U. L. Rev. 767, 783 (2003) ("Contracts that seek to prevent the use of information by withdrawing lawyers are likely to share a common fate with contracts that impose economic penalties on withdrawing lawyers who compete.").

[150]Hillman, "Loyalty in the Firm: A Statement of General Principles on the Duties of Partners Withdrawing From Law Firms" 55 Wash. & Lee L. Rev., 997, 1025-26 (1998).

[151]*Id.* at 1028-29.

Claims Relating to Partner Departure and Lateral Hiring VIII

The claims that may arise in the context of lateral hiring involving the departing partner and the acquiring firm generally fall into the category of "business torts." These causes of action relate to misuse of confidential information, breaches of fiduciary duties, tortious interference with another firm's relationships with employees or clients, and unfair competition. Although each of these claims have different elements, a lawsuit brought against departing partners and an acquiring firm would typically contain several or even all of these claims.

Cases imposing significant liability on lawyers because of the manner in which they handled their departure are rare but not unheard of, and usually involve numerous charges.[152] The few

---

[152]*California:* Reeves v. Hanlon, 33 Cal.4th 1140, 1145-1146, 17 Cal. Rptr.3d 289, 95 P.3d 513 (2004) (complaint asserting fourteen causes of action, including intentional interference with contractual relationships, interference with prospective business opportunity, conspiracy to interfere with prospective economic advantage, misappropriation of confidential information in violation of the UTSA, unauthorized use of a corporate car, and destruction of corporate property); Dickson, Carlson & Campillo v. Pole, 83 Cal. App.4th 436, 440 (2000) (alleging claims of breach of fiduciary duty, inducing intentional interference with prospective economic advantage, intentional interference with contractual relations, breach of contract,

cases that have been decided imposed significant liability on lawyers because of the manner in which they handled their departure. While these cases involved partners who left to form their own firms, the new firms were named defendants, and the principles espoused in those cases are applicable to lateral acquisitions.

Even in cases in which multiple fiduciary breaches were found, the courts have given fair warning that departures that are orchestrated in a way to give the departing partner and the acquiring firm an advantage or to injure the former firm pose significant risk. In an Illinois case, one of the major issues was whether the loss of a major client was caused by its solicitation by a departing partner who had been the chief client contact for 13 years.[153] Notwithstanding the client's testimony that he would never have remained with the firm if the attorney he had been dealing with was not there, the court refused to accept that the client's sentiments were anything more than speculation because the former firm had been deprived of any opportunity to try and retain his business by offering "more attractive fee arrangements."[154] In addition to securing the business of a major client for the new firm before giving notification of withdrawal, the court found that the departing partners also breached their fiduciary duties by: (1) voting and accepting large bonuses for themselves and their friends and family without disclosing that they would be leaving, stripping the firm of cash reserves, (2) using and removing confidential records related to the client, and (3) arranging for the mass exodus of firm employees before the notification date.[155]

In a California case,[156] the departing partners, one of whom was the chair of the plaintiff firm's litigation department and the other of whom was responsible for more than 500 client matters, engaged in unethical conduct for five months before their departure. They mounted a campaign against their former firm which included (1) accessing the plaintiff firm's password-protected computer database to print out confidential names, addresses, and

---

breach of implied covenant of good faith and fair dealing, unfair competition, and unjust enrichment).

Illinois: Dowd & Dowd, Ltd. v. Gleason, 352 Ill. App.3d 365, 287 Ill. Dec. 787, 816 N.E.2d 754 (.2004) (complaint alleging breach of fiduciary duty, breach of employment contract, tortious interference with prospective economic advantage and civil conspiracy.

See Sandburg, "Records Reveal Financial Life of Brobeck Before Its Collapse," New York Law Journal, p. 16 (Dec. 26, 2003), describing Brobeck, Phlager & Harrison, LLP against Clifford Chance Rogers & Wells, in which the claims asserted were breach of fiduciary duty, unfair competition, intentional interference with prospective business advantage, and tortious interference with a contract.

[153] Dowd & Dowd, Ltd. v. Gleason, 352 Ill. App.3d 365, 287 Ill. Dec. 787, 816 N.E.2d 754 (2004).

[154] *Id.*

[155] *Id.* The damage award totaled $2,464,889.46 and was comprised of the forfeiture of compensation/bonus payments, out-of-pocket damages, and two years of lost profits.

[156] Reeves v. Hanlon, 33 Cal.4th 1140, 17 Cal. Rptr.3d 289, 95 P.3d 513 (2004).

phone numbers of 2,200 clients, (2) cultivating employee discontent, (3) intentionally erasing extensive computer files in the plaintiff firm's computer server containing client documents and form files used by the plaintiff firm shortly before resigning, (4) abruptly resigning without notice, (5) leaving no status reports or lists of matters or deadlines on which they had been working, (6) personally soliciting the plaintiff firm's key employees on the evening of their resignations resulting in a loss to the plaintiff firm of nine employees over the next 60 days, six of whom joined the defendants' new firm, (7) not cooperating with the plaintiff firm on a notice to be sent, and (8) soliciting the plaintiff firm's clients, without offering them a choice of counsel and exploiting their lack of facility with English. All of this had been intentionally done to disrupt the firm's ongoing business and was calculated to cripple the firm's ability to provide legal services.[157]

A. Breach of Fiduciary Duty

The elements of a claim for breach of fiduciary duty are typically defined as (1) the existence of a fiduciary duty, (2) a breach of that duty, and (3) damages proximately caused by the breach to the plaintiff.[158]

---

[157]*Id.* The trial court found that defendants' conduct caused damage to plaintiffs in the total amount of $182,180.18, which it reduced to $150,000 pursuant to a stipulation between the parties.

[158]*See, e.g.,*

Second Circuit: Metropolitan West Asset Management, LLC v. Magnus, 2004 WL 1444868 (S.D.N.Y. 2004) (applying New York law) (to prevail on breach of fiduciary duty, a plaintiff must prove: (1) a fiduciary duty existing between the parties; (2) the defendant's breach of that duty; and (3) damages suffered by the plaintiff which were proximately caused by the breach).

California: Stanley v. Richmond, 35 Cal. App.4th 1070, 1086, 41 Cal. Rptr.2d 768 (1995) ("Breach of fiduciary duty, a tort distinct from professional negligence, has the following elements: (1) existence of a fiduciary duty; (2) breach of the fiduciary duty; and (3) damage proximately caused by the breach.").

District of Columbia: In re Belmar, 319 B.R. 748 (Bankr. D. Dist. Col. 2004) (Plaintiff must establish: (1) that defendant owed plaintiff a fiduciary duty; (2) that defendant breached that duty; and (3) that defendant's breach proximately caused an injury).

Illinois: AYH Holdings, Inc. v. Avreco, Inc., 357 Ill. App.3d 17, 2005 WL 736079 (Ill. App. 2005) ("To state a claim for breach of fiduciary duty, a plaintiff must establish: (1) a fiduciary duty on the part of the defendant; (2) the defendant's breach of that duty; and (3) damages that were proximately caused by the defendant's breach.")

Massachusetts: Qestec, Inc. v. Krummenacker, 367 F. Supp.2d 89 (D. Mass 2005) ("Claim of breach of fiduciary duty, under Massachusetts law, requires showing of (1) existence of fiduciary duty arising from relationship between parties, (2) breach of that duty, (3) damages and (4) causal relationship between breach and damages.").

See also: Hillman, "Loyalty in the Firm: A Statement of General Principles on the Duties of Partners Withdrawing from Law Firms" 55 Wash. & Lee L. Rev. 997, n. 65 (1998); *Restatement (Second) of Torts*, § 874 (1979).

The first element—the existence of a fiduciary duty—is a given in the context of a law partnership. As the Massachusetts Supreme Court held, "It is well settled that partners [in a law firm] owe each other a fiduciary duty of 'the utmost good faith and loyalty.' "[159] Indeed, the New York Court of Appeals noted it is fiduciary duties which "distinguish . . . law partnerships from bazaars."[160]

As to the second element, the kinds of activities that could be found to constitute fiduciary breaches in the context of lateral acquisitions include concealing or delaying taking on clients or matters so that they would be handled entirely at the new firm, handling a litigation or delaying settlement so as to enhance the benefits to the acquiring firm, obtaining and using confidential and proprietary information of the current firm, taking files belonging to the current firm, engaging in pre-resignation solicitation of clients, telling clients disparaging things about the current firm, encouraging clients to leave the current firm, and conspiring to leave the current firm in a way that is intended to damage the current firm.[161] Whether a breach has occurred is a question of fact.[162]

The degree of proof necessary for the third element—causation and damages—may vary, depending on the jurisdiction and the type of damages

---

[159]Meehan v. Shaughnessy, 404 Mass. 419, 433, 535 N.E.2d 1255 (1989). The same fiduciary duties apply where the firm is a professional corporation rather than a partnership. See, e.g., Lampert, Hausler & Rodman, P.C. v. Gallant, 2005 WL 109522, *5-6 (Super. Ct. Mass. 2005), *rev'd and remanded on other grounds*, 67 Mass. App. Ct. 1103 (2006).

[160]Graubard Mollen Dannett & Horowitz v. Moskowitz 86 N.Y.2d 112, 629 N.Y.S.2d 1009, 653 N.E.2d 1179 (1995).

[161]*See*:

Second Circuit: S & K Sales Co. v. Nike, 816 F.2d 843, 850 (2d Cir. 1987); Velo-Bind, Inc. v. Scheck, 485 F. Supp. 102, 109 (S.D.N.Y. 1979); A.H. Emery Co. v. Marcan Products Corp., 268 F. Supp. 289, 299, (S.D.N.Y. 1967), *aff'd*, 389 F.2d 11 (2d Cir.), *cert. denied*, 393 U.S. 835 (1968).

New York: Leo Silfen, Inc. v. Cream, 29 N.Y.2d 387, 391-392, 328 N.Y.S.2d 423, 427, 278 N.E.2d 636 (1972); Duane Jones Co., Inc. v. Burke, 306 N.Y. 172, 117 N.E.2d 237 (1954); A.S. Rampell, Inc. v. Hyster Co., 3 N.Y.2d 369, 165 N.Y.S.2d 475, 144 N.E.2d 371 (1957); Props for Today, Inc. v. Kaplan, 163 A.D.2d 177, 178, 558 N.Y.S.2d 38 (1st Dep't 1990); Foley v. D'Agostino, 21 A.D.2d 60, 248 N.Y.S.2d 121 (1964); Harry R. Defler Corp. v. Kleeman, 19 A.D.2d 396, 400-401, 243 N.Y.S.2d 930, 934 (1963), *aff'd*, 19 N.Y.2d 694, 278 N.Y.S.2d 883, 225 N.E.2d 569 (1967); David Fox & Sons, Inc. v. King Poultry Co., 47 Misc.2d 672, 262 N.Y.S.2d 983 (Sup.Ct. NY 1964), *aff'd*, 23 A.D.2d 966, 259 N.Y.S.2d 1012 (1st Dep't 1965).

[162]*See, e.g.*, Graubard Mollen Dannett & Horowitz v. Moskowitz, 86 N.Y.2d 112, 629 N.Y.S.2d 1009, 653 N.E.2d 1179 (1995) ("Factual variations can be crucial in determining whether an attorney's duties have been breached."); Burke v. Lakin Law Firm, PC, 2008 WL 64521, *4 (S.D. Ill. 2008) ("It is often difficult to draw the line between permissible and impermissible conduct" as to the arrangements a departing attorney may undertake to set up a competing firm; "[c]onsequently, whether a fiduciary duty has been violated depends on the particular facts involved in each case.")

sought. In acknowledgement of the public policy that a cause of action for breach of fiduciary duty "is a prophylactic rule intended to remove all incentive to breach—not simply to compensate for damages in the event of a breach," some jurisdictions have loosened the proof of causation and damage requirements.[163]

Under these lowered standards, a plaintiff need only prove that the breach is a "substantial cause" of the loss suffered by the plaintiff.[164] Thus, a plaintiff will not be required to show that but for the attorney's conduct, no loss would have occurred.[165] Instead, a plaintiff need only show some connection between the attorney's conduct and the subsequent loss and the defendant-attorney cannot disprove causation by showing that the losses might have resulted from other possible causes.[166] Other courts have opted to shift the burden of proving causation onto the attorneys accused of the breach.[167] Under this approach, the departing attorney must show that there is no causal link between the attorney's breach of duty and the firm's loss of business or profits.

Some courts have held that the long established "faithless servant" rule[168] also applies to partners, and thus a fiduciary may be required to forfeit

---

[163]*Second Circuit:* Milbank, Tweed, Hadley & McCloy v. Chan Cher Boon, 13 F.3d 537, 543 (2d Cir. 1994).

New York: Gibbs v. Breed, Abbott & Morgan, 271 A.D.2d 180, 710 N.Y.S.2d 578 (1st Dep't 2000).

[164]*Second Circuit:* Milbank, Tweed, Hadley & McCloy v. Boon, 13 F.3d 537 (2d Cir. 1994) (quoting ABKCO Music, Inc. v. Harrisongs Music, Ltd., 722 F.2d 988, 995-996 (2d Cir. 1983).

Eleventh Circuit: USA Interactive v. Dow Lohnes & Albertson, P.L.L.C., 328 F. Supp.2d 1294 (M.D. Fla. 2004) (applying Florida law).

California: Stanley v. Richmond, 35 Cal. App.4th 1070, 41 Cal. Rptr.2d 768 (1995).

New York: Gibbs v. Breed, Abbott & Morgan, 271 A.D.2d 180, 710 N.Y.S.2d 578 (1st Dep't 2000).

Wisconsin: Marshfield Machine Corp. v. Martin, 246 Wis.2d 668, 630 N.W.2d 275 (2001).

[165]*Id.*

[166]*Id.*

[167]*Sixth Circuit:* Ohio Drill & Tool Co. v. Johnson, 498 F.2d 186, 195 (6th Cir. 1974) (applying Ohio law).

Delaware: Fliegler v. Lawrence, 361 A.2d 218, 221 (Del. Supr. 1976).

Kansas: Newton v. Hornblower, Inc., 224 Kan. 506, 518, 582 P.2d 1136 (1978).

Massachusetts: Meehan v. Shaughnessy, 404 Mass. 419, 441, 535 N.E.2d 1255 (1989).

Texas: Huffington v. Upchurch, 532 S.W.2d 576, 579 (Tex. 1976).

[168]This rule requires a disloyal agent or employee to "forfeit any right to compensation for services" during the period of disloyalty. Murray v. Beard 102 N.Y. 505, 7 N.E. 553 (1886), quoted fifty years later in Lamdin v. Broadway Surface Advertising Corp., 272 N.Y. 133, 138-139, 5 N.E.2d 66 (N.Y. 1936). *See Restatement (Second) of Agency* § 469 ("agent is entitled to no compensation for conduct . . . which is a breach of his duty of loyalty").

compensation received during the period of the breach.[169] This remedy has been imposed without any requirement that the plaintiff prove either causation or actual damages to collect past compensation from the faithless fiduciary.[170] Other courts, however, have mitigated this harsh rule if the departing partner was still performing services of value to the former firm or working at his normal level of productivity notwithstanding the breach.[171]

In either case, generally courts have not been willing to extend the forfeiture rule to deprive a faithless partner of his or her return of capital or other interest in the partnership under the partnership agreement.[172] However, courts have approved adjustments in calculating the amounts due the departing partner under the partnership agreement based on the impact of his departure (with or without wrongful conduct) on the value of the former firm.[173] The New Jersey Supreme discussed this remedy in the context of what a departing partner is entitled to upon his departure:

> "We recognize that if a partner's departure will result in a decrease in the probability of a client's return and a consequent decrease in prospective earnings, that departure may decrease the value of the firm's goodwill. It would not be inappropriate therefore for law partners to take that specific effect into account in determining the shares due a departing partner."[174]

---

[169]*See, e.g.*, Dowd & Dowd, Ltd. v. Gleason, 352 Ill. App.3d 365, 287 Ill. Dec. 787, 816 N.E.2d 754 (2004), in which the court held that the departing partners could not "claim a right to retain the compensation earned while breaching their fiduciary duty to [the firm they left]"—nearly $850,000—even though "there was no indication that defendants did not work at the efficiency level or with the diligence that they had prior to deciding to leave" the firm. 352 Ill. App.3d at 385. Similarly, in Wenzel v. Hopper & Galliher, P.C., 779 N.E.2d 30, 46-48 (Ind. App. 2002) and 830 N.E.2d 996, 998-1002 (Ind. App. 2005), the court held that a departing shareholder-lawyer's "secret solicitation" of the firm's major client mandated forfeiture of his entire salary during the three month period of the solicitation—even though the solicitation was unsuccessful and the client remained at the firm.

[170]*Id.*

[171]*See, e.g.*, Meehan v. Shaughnessy, 404 Mass. 419, 535 N.E.2d 1255, 1263 (1989), in which the court rejected the former firm's contention that the departing partners forfeited their right to their capital contributions, their share of the dissolved partnership's profits, and six months compensation as an "extreme remedy." 404 Mass. at 438-439.

[172]*Id.*

[173]*See, e.g.*, Jacob v. Norris, McLaughlin & Marcus, 128 N.J. 10, 29, 607 A.2d 142, 152 (1992).

[174]*Id.*, 607 A.2d at 152. Similarly, the trial court in Gibbs v. Breed, Abbott & Morgan, 181 Misc.2d 346, 693 N.Y.S.2d 426 (Sup. Ct. NY 1999), *rev'd on other grounds* 271 A.D.2d 180, 710 N.Y.S.2d 578, 582-583 (1st Dep't 2000) noted that "[i]n a number of cases, it has been held that a partner whose wrong causes the dissolution of a partnership does not forfeit his entire interest but is entitled to receive it, less damages caused by the breach." (citing Staszak v. Romanik, 690 F.2d 578 (6th Cir. 1982)). In St. James Plaza v. Notey, 95 A.D.2d 804, 463 N.Y.S.2d 523 (1983), defendants were both partners and employees. Although they received unlawful kickbacks and had to account to the partnership for those funds, the court did not deprive defendants of their interest in the partnership.

B. Aiding and Abetting a Breach of Fiduciary Duty

Section 876(b) of the *Restatement (Second) of Torts* is widely cited as the basis for a cause of action for aiding and abetting breach of fiduciary duty. It provides:

> "For harm resulting to a third person from the tortious conduct of another, one is subject to liability if he . . . knows that the other's conduct constitutes a breach of duty and gives substantial assistance or encouragement to the other so to conduct himself."[175]

---

[175]*Restatement (Second) of Torts*, § 876(b) (American Law Institute 1979 Ed.). In Dale v. Ala Acquisitions, Inc., 203 F. Supp.2d 694, 701 (D. Miss., 2002), the court compiled a survey of the state of the law relating to a claim of aiding and abetting a breach of fiduciary duty and found: "Of the jurisdictions that have addressed § 876(b), twenty-eight have adopted a claim for aiding and abetting in some context." The court cited:

First Circuit: Invest Almaz v. Temple-Inland Forest Prods. Corp., 243 F.3d 57, 82-83 (1st Cir. 2001) (applying New Hampshire law).

Second Circuit: Centennial Textiles, Inc. v. Penn. Textile Corp., Inc., 227 B.R. 606, 611 (S.D.N.Y. 1998) (applying New York law).

Sixth Circuit: Aetna Casualty and Surety Co. v. Leahey Construction Co., Inc., 219 F.3d 519, 533-534 (6th Cir. 2000) (applying Ohio law); Lawyers Title Insurance Corp. v. United America Bank of Memphis, 21 F. Supp.2d 785, 795 (W.D. Tenn. 1998) (applying Tennessee law).

Tenth Circuit: Emig v. American Tobacco Co., Inc., 184 F.R.D. 379, 386 (D. Kan. 1998) (applying Kansas law).

Eleventh Circuit: Tew v. Chase Manhattan Bank, N.A., 728 F. Supp. 1551 (S.D. Fla.), *amended on reconsideration*, 741 F. Supp. 220 (1990) (applying Florida law).

District of Columbia Circuit: Halberstam v. Welch, 705 F.2d 472, 477-478 (D.C. Cir. 1983).

Arizona: Wells Fargo Bank v. Ariz. Laborers, Teamsters and Cement Masons Local No. 395 Pension Trust, 38 P.3d 12, 23 (Ariz. 2002).

California: Saunders v. Superior Court, 27 Cal. App.4th 832, 33 Cal. Rptr.2d 438, 446 (1994).

Colorado: Nelson v. Elway, 971 P.2d 245, 249-50, 98 CJ C.A.R. 1071 (Colo. App. 1998).

Connecticut: Feen v. Benefit Plan Administrators, Inc., 2000 WL 1398898, *10-11 (Conn. Super. 2000).

Delaware: Pipher v. Burr, 1998 Del. Super. LEXIS 26, No. C.A. 96 C-08-011, 1998 WL 110135, *9-10 (Del. Super. Jan 29, 1998).

Illinois: Sanke v. Bechina, 216 Ill. App.3d 962, 160 Ill. Dec. 258, 576 N.E.2d 1212, 1218-1219 (1991).

Iowa: Heick v. Bacon, 561 N.W.2d 45, 51-52 (Iowa 1997).

Maine: Hart Enters., Inc. v. Cheshire Sanitation, Inc., 1999 WL 33117189, *3 (D. Me. 1999).

Maryland: Alleco Inc. v. Harry & Jeanette Weinberg Found., Inc., 340 Md. 176, 665 A.2d 1038, 1049 (1995).

Massachusetts: Kurker v. Hill, 44 Mass. App. 184, 689 N.E.2d 833, 837 (1998).

Minnesota: Casino Res. Corp. v. Harrah's Entm't, Inc., 2002 WL 480968, *13 (D. Minn. 2002).

Missouri: Joseph v. Marriot International, Inc., 967 S.W.2d 624, 629-630 (Mo. App. 1998).

New Jersey: Herman v. Coastal Corp., 348 N.J. Super. 1, 791 A.2d 238, 253 (2002).

New Mexico: GCM, Inc. v. Kentucky. Central Life Insurance Co., 124 N.M. 186, 947 P.2d 143, 147-148 (1997).

Applying this standard, the elements of a cause of action for aiding and abetting a breach of fiduciary duty are generally held to consist of: (1) breach by a fiduciary of a duty owed to the plaintiff, (2) the defendant knowingly inducing or participating in that breach, and (3) damages suffered by the plaintiff as a result of the breach.[176] Inasmuch as the acquiring firm owes no fiduciary

---

Nevada: Dow Chemical Co. v. Mahlum, 114 Nev. 1468, 970 P.2d 98, 112-113 (Nev. 1998) (overruled in part on other grounds).

North Carolina: McMillan v. Mahoney, 99 N.C. App. 448, 393 S.E.2d 298, 300 (1990).

Oregon: Granewich v. Harding, 329 Ore. 47, 985 P.2d 788, 792-793 (1999).

Rhode Island: Groff v. Maurice,1993 WL 853801, *8 (R.I Super. Ct. 1993).

South Carolina: Future Group, II v. Nationsbank, 324 S.C. 89, 478 S.E.2d 45, 50 (S.C. 1996).

West Virginia: Estate of Janet Leigh Hough v. Estate of William Hough, 205 W. Va. 537, 519 S.E.2d 640, 648-49 (1999).

Wisconsin: Winslow v. Brown, 125 Wis.2d 327, 371 N.W.2d 417, 421-423 (1985).

The *Dale* court also found that "courts in three other states have held that the viability of such claims remains an open question." See:

Third Circuit: Daniel Boone Area School District v. Lehman Brothers, Inc., 187 F. Supp.2d 400, 413 (W.D. Penn. 2002).

Ninth Circuit: Unity House, Inc. v. North Pacific Investments, Inc., 918 F. Supp. 1384, 1390 (D. Haw. 1996).

Texas: Shinn v. Allen, 984 S.W.2d 308, 310 (Tex. App. 1998).

The *Dale* court further held that "Tennessee explicitly recognizes the tort of aiding and abetting fraud as provided for in *Restatement (Second) of Torts* § 876(b). See Lawyers Title Insurance Corp. v. United American Bank of Memphis, 21 F. Supp.2d 785, 795 (W.D. Tenn. 1998) ("Tennessee has adopted the *Restatement of Torts* § 876(b) theory of aiding and abetting, under which the plaintiff must show that 'the defendant knew that his companions' conduct constituted a breach of duty, and that he gave substantial assistance or encouragement to them in their acts' "), citing Cecil v. Hardin, 575 S.W.2d 268, 272 (Tenn. 1978)), and that "while the Mississippi Supreme Court ha[d] not expressly recognized the tort of aiding and abetting fraud," the court "predict[ed] that such a claim is viable under Mississippi law."

[176]*Second Circuit:* S & K Sales Co. v. Nike, Inc., 816 F.2d 843, 847-848 (2d Cir. 1987); *New York:* Shearson Lehman Brothers v. Bagley, 205 A.D.2d 467, 614 N.Y.S.2d 5 (1st Dep't 1994).

Other formulations of the standard include:

Third Circuit: Board of Trustees of Teamsters Local 863 Pension Fund v. Foodtown, Inc., 296 F.3d 164, 174 (3d Cir. 2002) ("In order to be found liable for aiding and abetting a breach of a fiduciary duty, one must demonstrate that the party knew that the other's conduct constituted a breach of a fiduciary duty and gave substantial assistance or encouragement to the other in committing that breach.").

Ninth Circuit: Goldin Assocs., L.L.C. ex rel. SmarTalk Teleservices, Inc. v. Donaldson, Lufkin & Jenrette Securities Corp., 2003 U.S. Dist. LEXIS 16798 (S.D.N.Y. 2003) (applying California law) ("Under California law, to be liable under an aiding and abetting theory, the third party must (i) be an active participant in the breach and (ii) participate in the breach for the purpose of advancing his or her interests or financial advantage," quoting Richardson v. Reliance National Indemnity Co., 2000 U.S. Dist. LEXIS 2838, No. C 99-2952 (CRB) (N.D. Cal. March 9, 2000).

California: City of Atascadero v. Merrill Lynch, Pierce, Fenner & Smith, Inc., 68 Cal. App.4th 445, 80 Cal. Rptr.2d 329, 342 (1998).

duty to the lateral's former firm, the first element necessarily depends on whether the departing partner committed a fiduciary breach.

The second element, "knowing participation" in the fiduciary's breach of trust, requires only a finding that the defendant "knew of the breach of duty and participated in it."[177] No finding of wrongful intent is necessary.[178] Courts differ, however, as to how extensive the conduct must be to satisfy this standard. The Second Circuit has held "the element of participation" to be "the essence of the claim,"[179] but it noted that the Ninth Circuit found liability when a competitor merely knowingly accepted the benefits of actions taken by disloyal employees.[180] The official comment to Section 876(b) of the *Restatement* sets forth a "substantial assistance" requirement:

Colorado: Nelson v. Elway, 971 P.2d 245, 249-50, 98 CJ C.A.R. 1071 (Colo. App. 1998) ("The elements of the tort of aiding and abetting a breach of fiduciary duty include: (1) breach by a fiduciary of a duty owed to a plaintiff, (2) a defendant's knowing participation in the breach, and (3) damages. . . . Also, *Restatement (Second) of Torts* § 876(b) (1977), upon which the tort is premised, includes as an additional element that a defendant must give substantial assistance to the other's breach.")

Massachussetts: Spinner v. Nutt, 417 Mass. 549, 631 N.E.2d 542 (1994) ("[the plaintiff must show that the defendant knew of the breach and actively participated in it such that he or she could not reasonably be held to have acted in good faith.")

New Jersey: Judson v. Peoples Bank and Trust Co., 25 N.J. 17, 25, 134 A.2d 761, 767 (1957) ("A person is liable with another if he 'knows that the other's conduct constitutes a breach of duty and gives substantial assistance or encouragement to the other so to conduct himself.' ")

Pennsylvania: Koken v. Steinberg, 825 A.2d 723, 731-32 (Pa. 2003) ("Section 876 is a viable cause of action in Pennsylvania" and requires that "a defendant must render substantial assistance to another to accomplish a tortious act"). *But see,* Daniel Boone Area School District v. Lehman Brothers, Inc., 187 F. Supp.2d 400, 413 (W.D. Pa 2002), in which the court dismissed an aiding and abetting claim under the *Restatement (Second) Of Torts* § 876(b) because "the Pennsylvania Supreme Court has not yet adopted § 876(b) as the law of Pennsylvania . . . and the adoption of § 876(b) would represent a significant expansion of Pennsylvania tort liability." *And see,* Adelphia Recovery Trust v. Bank of America, N.A. 2008 WL 217057, 10 (S.D.N.Y. 2008), *adhered to on reconsideration,* 2008 WL 1959542 (S.D.N.Y. 2008) (Although "the lower state and federal courts in Pennsylvania are not consistent with each other" as to whether aiding and abetting a breach of fiduciary duty would be recognized by the Pennsylvania Supreme Court as a tort," "a relatively recent decision by the Third Circuit, *Huber v. Taylor,* 469 F.3d 67, 79 (3d Cir. 2006), assumes the existence in Pennsylvania of the tort of aiding and abetting the breach of fiduciary duty.")

[177]Holmes v. Young, 885 P.2d 305 (Colo. App. 1994). *See also,* S & K Sales Co. v. Nike, Inc., 816 F.2d 843, 848 (2d Cir. 1987).

[178]Holmes v. Young, 885 P.2d 305 (Colo. App. 1994).

[179]S & K Sales Co. v. Nike, Inc., 816 F.2d 843, 848 (2d Cir. 1987).

[180]*Id.,* citing American Republic Insurance Co. v. Union Fidelity Life Insurance Co., 470 F.2d 820, 824-826 (9th Cir. 1972). In the Ninth Circuit case, the court held that the new employer:

"knew of the strong likelihood that any use [the departing employee] made of these leads would be in derogation of the rights of [the former employer]. Yet when it appeared that [the departing employee] was soliciting former customers of [the former employer], [the new employer] made no effort to check further on

"Advice or encouragement to act operates as a moral support to a tortfeasor and if the act encouraged is known to be tortious it has the same effect upon the liability of the adviser as participation or physical assistance. If the encouragement or assistance is a substantial factor in causing the resulting tort, the one giving it is himself a tortfeasor and is responsible for the consequences of the other's act."

"Participation" and "substantial assistance" have been defined as affirmatively assisting the fiduciary in the breach, helping conceal the breach, or failing to act when required to do so as to enable the breach to proceed.[181] The *Restatement (Second) of Torts* points to five factors as an aid to determining whether "the assistance of or participation by the defendant may be so slight that he is not liable for the act of the other:" (1) the nature of the act encouraged, (2) the amount of assistance given by the defendant, (3) his presence or absence at the time of the tort, (4) his relation to the other, and (5) his state of mind.[182] Some courts have suggested an additional factor: the duration of the assistance provided.[183]

With respect to the question as to what constitutes sufficient "knowledge" for liability to be found, the *Restatement's* requirement of actual knowledge has been "widely adopted."[184] Indeed, the New York courts have repeatedly held that actual knowledge of the breach by the fiduciary is required where the claimed aider and abettor has no independent fiduciary duty to the plaintiff, as would be the case with respect to an acquiring law firm.[185] This has

---

his activities nor to prevent [the departing employees] from enlisting other salesmen of [the former employer] to work for [the new employer]. [The new employer] received great economic benefits from [the departing employee]'s new agency. Ignorance and inaction will not suffice to avoid responsibility for [the former employer's] losses."

[181]Kolbeck v. LIT America, Inc., 939 F. Supp. 240, 247 (S.D.N.Y. 1996), *aff'd*, 152 F.3d 918 (2d Cir. 1998). *See also*, White v. Kenneth Warren & Son, Ltd., 2000 WL 91920, *8 (N.D. Ill. 2000).

[182]*Restatement (Second) of Torts* § 876 (b), official comment.

[183]*Eighth Circuit:* In re TMJ Implants Prod. Liab. Litig., 113 F.3d 1484, 1495 (8th Cir. 1997).
District of Columbia Circuit: Halberstam v. Welch, 705 F.2d 472, 484 (D.C. Cir. 1983).
See Willis, "Annual Survey Of South Carolina Law: Tort Law to (b) or Not to (b): The Future of Aider and Abettor Liability in South Carolina," 51 S.C. L. Rev. 1045 (2000).

[184]*See, e.g.*, In re Consolidated Welfare Fund ERISA Litigation v. Empire Blue Cross/Blue Shield, 856 F. Supp. 837, 842 (S.D.N.Y. 1994). See also, Invest Almaz v. Temple Inland Forest Products Corporation, 243 F.3d 57 (1st Cir. 2001).

[185]In Kolbeck v. LIT America, Inc., 939 F. Supp. 240, 245 (S.D.N.Y. 1996), *aff'd*, 152 F.3d 918 (2d Cir. 1998), the court cited numerous cases for the proposition that "New York common law, which controls the analysis here, has not adopted a constructive knowledge standard for imposing aiding and abetting liability. Rather, New York courts and federal courts in this district, have required actual knowledge." It further noted that in applying the law of other states, New York courts have required proof of actual knowledge, citing In re Consolidated Welfare Fund ERISA Litigation, 856 F. Supp. 837, 842 (S.D.N.Y. 1994) (applying California law)

also been the rule applied by most other courts,[186] though there has been some discussion of whether constructive knowledge of the breach would suffice.[187]

C. Civil Conspiracy

The elements for a cause of action for civil conspiracy are: "(1) two or more persons, (2) an object to be accomplished, (3) a meeting of the minds on the object or course of action, (4) an unlawful overt act, and (5) damages as the proximate result."[188] The distinguishing feature of the conspiracy claim is an

---

("It is clear that liability for aiding and abetting a tort cannot attach absent actual knowledge of the underlying tort."); Terrydale Liquidating Trust v. Barness, 611 F. Supp. 1006, 1027 (S.D.N.Y. 1984) (applying Missouri law) ("[L]iability cannot be imposed absent a showing that the defendants had actual knowledge of tortious conduct by the primary wrongdoer."); Samuel M. Feinberg Testamentary Trust v. Carter, 652 F. Supp. 1066, 1082 (S.D.N.Y. 1987) ("Actual knowledge, not mere notice or unreasonable awareness, is . . . essential."); See Constantin Associates v. Kapetas, 17 Misc.3d 1137(A), 2007 WL 4294732, *4 (Sup. Ct. NY 2007).

[186]*See, e.g.*:
   Second Circuit: Dubai Islamic Bank v. Citibank, N.A., 256 F. Supp.2d 158 (S.D.N.Y. 2003).
   Fourth Circuit: Multi-Channel TV Cable Co. v. Charlottesville Quality Cable Operating Company, 108 F.3d 522 (4th Cir. 1997).
   Colorado: Holmes v. Young, 885 P.2d 305, 310 (Colo. App. 1994).

[187]*See* Holmes v. Young, 885 P.2d 305, 310 (Colo. App. 1994), which compared Terrydale Liquidating Trust v. Barness, 611 F. Supp. 1006 (S.D.N.Y. 1984), in which actual knowledge was required under the circumstances present with Diduck v. Kaszycki & Sons Contractors, Inc., 974 F.2d 270 (2d Cir. 1992), in which defendant was "on notice" that the breach may have been occurring and therefore a duty to investigate was triggered.

[188]Nelson v. Elway, 971 P.2d 245, 249-50, 98 CJ C.A.R. 1071 (Colo. App. 1998). See also, Procom Services, Inc. v. Deal, 2003 U.S. Dist. LEXIS 1956 (N.D. Tex. 1956). Other formulations of the standard include:
   California: Saunders v. Superior Court, 27 Cal. App.4th 832, 33 Cal. Rptr.2d 438, 446 (1994) ("The elements of a civil conspiracy are the formation and operation of the conspiracy and damage resulting to plaintiff from an act done in furtherance of the common design. . . . In order to state a cause of action for civil conspiracy, a plaintiff must show that two or more persons combined or agreed with intent to do an unlawful act or to do an otherwise lawful act by unlawful means. Proof of malice, i.e., an intent to injure, is essential in proof of a conspiracy").
   Illinois: Dames & Moore v. Baxter & Woodman, Inc., 21 F. Supp.2d 817, 824 (N.D. Ill. 1998) ("To state a claim for civil conspiracy, a plaintiff must allege: (1) an agreement between at least two people for the purpose of accomplishing some unlawful purpose or some lawful purpose by unlawful means; and (2) at least one tortious act by one of the co-conspirators in furtherance of the agreement").
   New York: Anesthesia Associates of Mount Kisco, LLP v. Northern Westchester Hosp. Center 2009 WL 324047, *4 (2 Dep't 2009) ("Although an independent cause of action for civil conspiracy is not recognized in this State . . . a plaintiff may plead the existence of a conspiracy in order to connect the actions of the individual defendants with an actionable, underlying tort and establish that those actions were part of a common scheme" . . . "The allegation of conspiracy carries no greater burden, but also no less, than to assert adequately common action for a common purpose by common agreement or understanding among a group, from which common responsibility derives." [Citations omitted]).

agreement with respect to the commission of the fiduciary breaches. By virtue of the agreement, the non-fiduciary assumes liability for the acts of the fiduciary.[189] Thus, the difference between the claims of conspiracy and aiding and abetting is that the former requires an agreement with respect to the breach but no overt act in furtherance thereof on the part of the non-fiduciary, whereas the latter requires no agreement but participation in the breach. Moreover, some authorities hold that, unlike an aiding and abetting claim, a conspiracy claim requires "proof of an unlawful intent."[190]

Because civil conspiracy is a "derivative tort,"[191] there must be "some underlying tort for which the plaintiff seeks to hold at least one of the named defendants liable."[192] However, there is a split in authority as to (1) whether both conspirators must be "legally capable of committing the tort," i.e., that both owe "a duty to plaintiff,"[193] or (2) whether the fact that the non-fiduciary could not commit such a breach permits the non-fiduciary to escape liability for a co-conspirator's unlawful acts.[194] Other courts have enunciated an exception to the rule prohibiting suit against a non-fiduciary conspirator due to the lack

---

[189] *Third Circuit:* Daniel Boone Area School District v. Lehman Brothers, Inc., 187 F. Supp.2d 400, 412 n.13 (W.D. Pa. 2002) ("One may be a conspirator in a civil conspiracy without oneself committing any 'tortious act.' Liability for civil conspiracy is available because the tortious acts of one co-conspirator may be imputed to other co-conspirators.").

California: Saunders v. Superior Court, 27 Cal. App.4th 832, 33 Cal. Rptr.2d 438, 446 (1994).

[190] Nelson v. Elway, 971 P.2d 245, 249-50, 98 CJ C.A.R. 1071 (Colo. App. 1998).

[191] Procom Services, Inc. v. Deal, 2003 U.S. Dist. LEXIS 1956 (N.D. Tex. 1956) ("Civil conspiracy is not an independent tort; rather, it is a theory by which liability is imposed on " 'persons who, although not actually committing a tort themselves, share with the immediate tortfeasors a common plan or design in its perpetration.' ").

[192] *Id.*

[193] 1-800 Contacts, Inc. v. Steinberg, 107 Cal. App.4th 568, 590; 132 Cal. Rptr.2d 789, 807 (2003) ("tort liability arising from conspiracy presupposes that the coconspirator is legally capable of committing the tort, i.e., that he or she owes a duty to plaintiff . . . and is potentially subject to liability for breach of that duty."); Kidron v. Movie Acquisition Corp., 40 Cal. App.4th 1571, 1597, 47 Cal. Rptr.2d 752 (1995) ("[a] nonfiduciary cannot conspire to breach a duty owed only by a fiduciary.").

Some California Courts have rejected this absolute prohibition and have held that California law permits a plaintiff to sue a third party for conspiracy to breach a fiduciary duty if the third party was acting for personal gain or in furtherance of his or her own financial advantage. Richardson v. Reliance National Indemnity Co., 2000 U.S. Dist. LEXIS 2838 (N.D. Cal. 2000); City of Atascadero v. Merrill Lynch, Pierce, Fenner & Smith, Inc. 68 Cal. App.4th 445, 464, 80 Cal. Rptr.2d 329 (1998).

[194] *See,* Daniel Boone Area School District v. Lehman Brothers, Inc., 187 F. Supp.2d 400, 411 (W.D. Pa. 2002) ("Just because Lehman could not itself commit any unlawful act by selling derivatives, that does not mean that it could not be liable for a civil conspiracy with Black if Black's purchase of the derivatives were unlawful.").

of any duty when the third party was acting for personal gain or in further-ance of his own financial advantage.[195]

D. Tortious Interference Claims

There are two types of tortious interference claims: tortious interference with a contract and tortious interference with a prospective economic advantage or business relationship. In the context of lateral hiring, these claims can arise with respect to both clients and employees.

1. Tortious Interference with Contract

The elements of a claim of tortious interference with contract are (1) the ex-istence of a valid contract between the plaintiff and a third party, (2) the de-fendant's knowledge of that contract, (3) the defendant's intentional procur-ing of the breach, and (4) damages.[196]

Given the requirements of a contract and a procurement of a breach, this claim would only have application in the context of a lateral acquisition when there was an agreement between a lateral and his former firm which was for

---

[195]*Ninth Circuit:* Richardson v. Reliance National Indemnity Co., 2000 U.S. Dist. LEXIS 2838 (N.D. Cal. 2000).

California: City of Atascadero v. Merrill Lynch, Pierce, Fenner & Smith, Inc., 68 Cal. App.4th 445, 80 Cal. Rptr.2d 329 (1998).

See also, Everest Investors 8 v. Whitehall Real Estate Partnership XI, 100 Cal. App.4th 1102, 1104, 123 Cal. Rptr.2d 297 (2002):

> "The question on this appeal is whether a nonfiduciary defendant can be liable for conspiring with a fiduciary defendant to breach the fiduciary's duty to the plaintiff. The answer, in our view, is sometimes yes and sometimes no. When the nonfiduciary is an agent or employee of the fiduciary, the nonfiduciary is enti-tled to the benefit of the "agent's immunity rule" (and thus not liable on a con-spiracy theory) unless the nonfiduciary was acting for its own benefit. If the nonfiduciary is neither an employee nor agent of the fiduciary, it is not liable to the plaintiff on a conspiracy theory because a nonfiduciary is legally incapable of committing the tort underlying the claim of conspiracy (breach of fiduciary duty)."

[196]*See, e.g.,*

Seventh Circuit: Borowski v. DePuy, Inc., A Division of Boehringer Mannheim Co., 850 F.2d 297 (7th Cir. 1988).

Eighth Circuit: Sawheny v. Pioneer Hi-Bred International Inc., 93 F.3d 1401 (8th Cir. 1996).

Florida: Salit v. Ruden, McKlosky, Smith, Schuster & Russell, 742 So.2d 381 (Fla. App. 1999).

New York: Foster v. Churchill, 87 N.Y.2d 744, 749-750, 642 N.Y.S.2d 583, 665 N.E.2d 153 (1996).

a specific term and was not terminable at will.[197] This is not typically the case in law firms either between firms and partners, firms and employees, or firms and clients. If such an agreement did exist, however, the element of knowledge could be shown by evidence that the lateral advised the acquiring firm that he had a contract with the prior firm or that the lateral actually gave the acquiring firm a copy of that contract. Evidence that the acquiring firm took actions to procure a breach of the lateral's contract could include offering better terms or other incentives[198] or agreeing to defend and indemnify the lateral in the event that the prior firm did sue.[199]

A defense to a claim of tortious interference with contract is economic justification, unless there is a showing of malice or illegality.[200]

2. *Tortious Interference with Prospective Economic Advantage*

A claim for tortious interference can also be brought with respect to at-will employees or client relationships. In both instances, the relationship can be terminated at any time, and tort claims have been sustained in the law firm context when there has been interference with the relationship.[201] Because it is essentially a future relationship that is being interfered with, the courts have generally permitted such claims under a theory of tortious interference with a prospective economic advantage or business relationships.[202]

There are two main formulations of this claim. The first is based on Section 766B of the *Restatement (Second) of Torts* and only requires that the interference be both intentional and improper.[203] It has been adopted by a

---

[197]There is some authority, however, which recognizes a tort action for interference with a contract even if the contract is unenforceable. *See, e.g.*, Saunders v. Superior Court, 27 Cal. App.4th 832, 33 Cal. Rptr.2d 438 (1994), citing Pacific Gas & Electric Co. v. Bear Stearns & Co., 50 Cal.3d 1118, 1127-1128, 270 Cal. Rptr. 1, 791 P.2d 587 (1990).

[198]State Enterprises, Inc. v. Southridge Cooperative Section 1, Inc., 18 A.D.2d 226, 227-228, 238 N.Y.S.2d 724, 726 (1963).

[199]Indemnity arrangements (as well as financial incentives) have been held to constitute compelling proof of intentional interference with contract. Ecolab Inc. v. K.P. Laundry Machinery, Inc., 656 F. Supp. 894, 897 (S.D.N.Y. 1987) ("There can be little doubt that the indemnification agreements, as well as the large salaries, were offered to [plaintiff's] employees to encourage them to breach their contractual obligation. . . .").

[200]Foster v. Churchill, 87 N.Y.2d 744, 749-750, 642 N.Y.S.2d 583, 665 N.E.2d 153 (1996).

[201]*California:* Reeves v. Hanlon, 33 Cal.4th 1140, 17 Cal. Rptr.3d 289, 95 P.3d 513 (2004).

    Illinois: Dowd & Dowd, Ltd. v. Gleason, 352 Ill. App.3d 365, 287 Ill. Dec. 787, 816 N.E.2d 754 (2004).

[202]*See, e.g.*, Reeves v. Hanlon, 33 Cal.4th 1140, 17 Cal. Rptr.3d 289 95 P.3d 513 (2004).

[203]*Restatement (Second) of Torts* § 766B, "Intentional Interference with Prospective Contractual Relation."

> "One who intentionally and improperly interferes with another's prospective contractual relation (except a contract to marry) is subject to liability to the other for the pecuniary harm resulting from loss of the benefits of the relation,

majority of jurisdictions.[204] The second formulation, which has been adopted by a more limited number of jurisdictions, including California,[205] New

---

whether the interference consists of (a) inducing or otherwise causing a third person not to enter into or continue the prospective relation or (b) preventing the other from acquiring or continuing the prospective relation."

[204]*See, e.g.:*

Florida: Ferguson Transportation, Inc. v. North American Van Lines, Inc., 687 So.2d 821, 822 (Fla. Sup. 1996) ("As a general rule, an action for tortious interference with a business relationship requires a business relationship evidenced by an actual and identifiable understanding or agreement which in all probability would have been completed if the defendant had not interfered.").

Illinois: Voyles v. Sandia Mortgage Corporation, 196 Ill.2d 288, 300-301, 256 Ill. Dec. 289, 751 N.E.2d 1126 (2001) ("To state a cause of action for intentional interference with prospective economic advantage, a plaintiff must allege (1) a reasonable expectancy of entering into a valid business relationship, (2) the defendant's knowledge of the expectancy, (3) an intentional and unjustified interference by the defendant that induced or caused a breach or termination of the expectancy, and (4) damage to the plaintiff resulting from the defendant's interference."); Edelman, Combs and Latturner v. Hinshaw and Culbertson, 338 Ill. App.3d 156, 169, 273 Ill. Dec. 149, 788 N.E.2d 740 (2003); Fellhauer v. City of Geneva, 142 Ill.2d 495, 154 Ill. Dec 649, 568 N.E.2d 870 (1991).

New Jersey: Macdougall v. Weichert, 144 N.J. 380, 677 A.2d 162, 174 (1996) (To maintain an action for tortious interference (1) "the complaint must allege facts that show some protectable right—a prospective economic or contractual relationship . . . [(2)] the complaint must allege facts claiming that the interference was done intentionally and with malice . . ." which "is defined to mean that the harm was inflicted intentionally and without justification or excuse . . . [(3)] the complaint must allege facts leading to the conclusion that the interference caused the loss of the prospective gain," i.e. "if there had been no interference[,] there was a reasonable probability that the victim of the interference would have received the anticipated economic benefits" and (4) "the complaint must allege that the injury caused damage.") (Internal quotations omitted).

[205]Reeves v. Hanlon, 33 Cal.4th 1140, 17 Cal. Rptr.3d 289, 95 P.3d 513 (2004). *See* Korea Supply Co. v. Lockheed Martin Corp., 29 Cal.4th 1134, 1164-1165, 131 Cal. Rptr.2d 29, 63 P.3d 937 (2003), stating that the elements of the tort of intentional interference with prospective economic advantage are:

"(1) an economic relationship between the plaintiff and some third party, with the probability of future economic benefit to the plaintiff; (2) the defendant's knowledge of the relationship; (3) intentional acts on the part of the defendant designed to disrupt the relationship; (4) actual disruption of the relationship; and (5) economic harm to the plaintiff proximately caused by the acts of the defendant." 29 Cal.4th at 1159. (Citations omitted.)

The court went on to make clear that the third element (intentional acts) of this standard requires:

"(1) that the defendant engaged in an independently wrongful act, and (2) that the defendant acted either with the desire to interfere or the knowledge that interference was certain or substantially certain to occur as a result of its action. . . . Unlike California, the *Restatement Second of Torts* does not require a plaintiff to plead that a defendant engaged in an independently wrongful act in order to show 'improper' interference. [This requirement] "narrowly defines actionable conduct" and "differentiates California law from that of other states and the *Restatement Second of Torts*." 29 Cal.4th at 1160.

York,[206] and Texas,[207] has the more stringent requirement that the defendant must have accomplished the interference by "wrongful means" or engaged in an independently wrongful act, i.e., an act "proscribed by some constitutional, statutory, regulatory, common law, or other determinable legal standard."[208] "Wrongful means" can be established when the alleged means employed consisted of fraudulent representations, threats or violation of "a duty of fidelity" owed "by reason of a relationship of confidence."[209] Thus, the other torts typically asserted in a lawsuit against an acquiring firm, such as aiding and abetting a breach of fiduciary duty or entering into a conspiracy with respect to such a breach, can be sufficient to constitute the requisite underlying tort.[210]

The California Supreme Court held that a law firm may recover for interference with the employment contracts of its at-will employees by another employer when the acquiring firm engages in an independently wrongful act

---

[206]Carvel Corp. v. Noonan, 3 N.Y.3d 182, 785 N.Y.S.2d 359, 818 N.E.2d 1100 (2004).

[207]Wal-Mart Stores, Inc. v. Sturges, 52 S.W.3d 711, 713, 44 Tex. Sup. Ct. J. 486 (Tex. Sup. 2001):

> "[W]e conclude that to establish liability for interference with a prospective contractual or business relation the plaintiff must prove that it was harmed by the defendant's conduct that was either independently tortious or unlawful. By 'independently tortious' we mean conduct that would violate some other recognized tort duty; . . . we do not mean that the plaintiff must be able to prove an independent tort. Rather, we mean only that the plaintiff must prove that the defendant's conduct would be actionable under a recognized tort."

[208]Other cases in various jurisdictions in which courts have required "wrongful means" as an element of a claim for tortious interference with prospective relationships include:
Third Circuit: Franklin Music Co. v. American Broadcasting Cos., 616 F.2d 528 (3d Cir. 1979) (applying Pennsylvania law).
Sixth Circuit: United Rentals (North America), Inc. v. Keizer, 355 F.3d 399 (6th Cir 2004) (applying Michigan law) ("An essential element of a claim for tortious interference with contract, tortious interference with business relations and civil conspiracy is that the alleged tortious conduct be wrongful.").
Michigan: Trepel v. Pontiac Osteopathic Hospital, 135 Mich. App. 361, 354 N.W.2d 341, 347 (1984) (Tort of intentional interference with contract or with business relations requires a showing of "illegal, unethical or fraudulent conduct in addition to intentional interference").
North Dakota: Trade 'N Post, L.L.C. v. World Duty Free Americas, Inc., 2001 ND 116, 628 N.W.2d 707 (2001) ("[W]e agree with the growing body of cases which hold that, in order to recover for wrongful interference with business, the plaintiff must prove the defendant's conduct was independently tortious or otherwise unlawful.").

[209]Guard-Life Corp. v. S. Parker Hardware Manufacturing Corp. 50 N.Y.2d 183, 428 N.Y.S.2d 628, 634, 406 N.E.2d 445 (1980). See also, A.S. Rampell, Inc. v. Hyster Co., 3 N.Y.2d 369, 165 N.Y.S.2d 475, 144 N.E.2d 371 (1957); Duane Jones Co. v. Burke, 306 N.Y. 172, 117 N.E.2d 237 (1954).

[210]Franklin Music Co. v. American Broadcasting Cos., 616 F.2d 528, 545 (3d Cir. 1979) (applying Pennsylvania law) ("Encouraging a breach of fiduciary duty and civil conspiracy are, after all, wrongs. If those wrongs are related to the interference with employment, as on this record they can be, the civil tort of interference with a prospective relationship with an at-will employee under Pennsylvania law has been made out.")

that induces an at-will employee to leave his previous employment.[211] In so doing, the court noted that "[u]nder this standard, a defendant is not subject to liability for intentional interference if the interference consists merely of extending a job offer that induces an employee to terminate his or her at-will employment."[212] It then held that the standard is satisfied when the acquiring employer purposely engages in unlawful acts that cripple the prior employer's business operations and causes the prior employer's personnel to terminate their at-will employment contracts.[213]

In some states, including New York, liability can alternatively be established by proof that the defendant acted with malice or evil motive.[214] Malice, for these purposes, means engaging in conduct "for the sole purpose of inflicting intentional harm."[215] In the case of competitors, acting in one's "normal economic self-interest" is not malice."[216] However, whether a competitor had an economic interest and, if so, whether it was motivated by that economic interest or by a desire to injure the plaintiff's business are issues of fact.[217] The *Restatement (Second) of Torts* provides a guide to making that determination:

> "The question whether [economic] pressure is proper is answered in the light of the circumstances in which it is exerted, the object sought to be accomplished by the actor, the degree of coercion involved, the extent of the harm that it threatens, the effect upon neutral parties drawn into the

---

[211]Reeves v. Hanlon, 33 Cal.4th 1140, 17 Cal. Rptr.3d 289, 95 P.3d 513 (2004).

[212]*Id.*, 33 Cal.4th at 1153.

[213]*Id.*, 33 Cal.4th at 1155.

[214]Guard-Life Corp. v. S. Parker Hardware Manufacturing Corp. 50 N.Y.2d 183, 428 N.Y.S.2d 628, 632, 406 N.E.2d 445 (1980). See also, State Enterprises, Inc. v. Southridge Cooperative Section 1, Inc., 18 A.D.2d 226, 238 N.Y.S.2d 724, 726; Avon Products, Inc. v. Berson, 206 Misc. 900, 135 N.Y.S.2d 867 (N.Y. Sup. 1954); Revlon Products Corp. v. Bernstein, 204 Misc. 80, 119 N.Y.S.2d 60 (N.Y. Sup. 1953).

The court in Mino v. Clio School District, 255 Mich. App. 60, 661 N.W.2d 586, 597 (2003) also noted that a lawful act done with malice can constitute actionable interference:

> "The elements of tortious interference with a business relationship are the existence of a valid business relationship or expectancy, knowledge of the relationship or expectancy on the part of the defendant, an intentional interference by the defendant inducing or causing a breach or termination of the relationship or expectancy, and resultant damage to the plaintiff. To establish that a lawful act was done with malice and without justification, the plaintiff must demonstrate, with specificity, affirmative acts by the defendant that corroborate the improper motive of the interference. Where the defendant's actions were motivated by legitimate business reasons, its actions would not constitute improper motive or interference."

[215]Carvel Corp. v. Noonan, 3 N.Y.3d 182, 785 N.Y.S.2d 359, 818 N.E.2d 1100 (2004).

[216]*Id.*

[217]Saunders v. Superior Court, 27 Cal. App.4th 832, 33 Cal. Rptr.2d 438, 446 (1994).

situation, the effects upon competition, and the general reasonableness and appropriateness of this pressure as a means of accomplishing the actor's objective."[218]

E. Raiding

When an acquiring firm attempts to injure a competing firm by appropriating a large number of its employees, it may be held liable. In an early case in which an employer sought to enjoin workers from conspiring to induce a large number of employees to leave the employer's business at the same time, the Supreme Court stated that if the conspiring workers had been competitors of the employer, their acts would have exceeded the "bounds of fair play."[219] As the court explained:

> "Certainly, if a competing trader should endeavor to draw custom from his rival, not by offering better or cheaper goods, employing more competent salesmen, or displaying more attractive advertisements, but by persuading the rival's clerks to desert him under circumstances rendering it difficult or embarrassing for him to fill their places, a court of equity would grant an injunction to restrain this conduct."[220]

Indeed, arranging for a mass exodus of employees and unfairly impairing the ability of a law firm to retain its employees are key aspects of the far more extensive wrongful conduct the courts rely on in finding liability.[221] In other businesses where poaching employees was extensive and accompanied by other wrongful conduct, the courts have not hesitated to impose liability.[222] In a seminal New York case in which the defendants threatened mass exodus of an employer's customers and a majority of its key personnel unless the em-

---

[218]*Restatement (Second) of Torts* § 767.

[219]Hitchman Coal & Coke Co. v. Mitchell, 245 U.S. 229, 259, 38 S.Ct. 65, 62 L.Ed. 260 (1917).

[220]*Id.*, 245 U.S. at 259.

[221]*California:* Reeves v. Hanlon, 33 Cal.4th 1140, 17 Cal. Rptr.3d 289, 95 P.3d 513 (2004).
     Illinois: Dowd & Dowd, Ltd. v. Gleason, 352 Ill. App.3d 365, 287 Ill. Dec. 787, 816 N.E.2d 754 (2004).

[222]*Ninth Circuit:* American Republic Insurance Co. v. Union Fidelity Life Insurance Co., 470 F.2d 820 (9th Cir. 1972); Alexander & Alexander Benefits Services, Inc. v. Benefits Brokers & Consultants, Inc., 756 F. Supp 1408 (D. Ore.1991).
     Colorado: Jet Courier Service, Inc. v. Mulei, 771 P.2d 486 (Colo. Sup. 1989).
     Illinois: ABC Transnational Transport, Inc. v. Aeronautics Forwarders, Inc., 90 Ill. App.3d 817, 234 N.E.2d 1299 (1968).
     New York: Duane Jones Co., Inc. v. Burke, 306 N.Y. 172, 117 N.E.2d 237 (1953); American League Baseball Club of New York, Inc. v. Pasquel, 187 Misc. 230, 232-233, 63 N.Y.S.2d 537 (N.Y. Sup. 1946).

ployer ceded its business to the defendants, a jury was entitled to find that plaintiff's losses were a proximate result of defendants' conduct.[223] As a result, the employer "was entitled to recover as damages the amount of loss sustained by it, including opportunities for profit on the accounts diverted from it through defendants' conduct."[224]

F. Unfair Competition

Causes of action for unfair competition may have either a common law or statutory basis. In explaining a common law claim, one court stated:

> "The modern view as to the law of unfair competition does not rest solely on the ground of direct competitive injury, but on the broader principle that property rights of commercial value are to be and will be protected from any form of unfair invasion or infringement and from any form of commercial immorality."[225]

The court held that a separate and independent cause of action for unfair competition is stated when defendants have conspired to "profit from the labor skill, expenditures, name and reputation" of another.[226]

An illustration of a statutory claim is the very broad California statute which defines unfair competition as "any unlawful, unfair or fraudulent business act or practice."[227] The "unlawful" practices prohibited by the statute are any practices forbidden by law, be it civil or criminal, federal, state, or mu-

---

[223]Duane Jones Co., Inc. v. Burke, 306 N.Y. 172, 117 N.E.2d 237 (1953).

[224]*Id.* See also, American League Baseball Club of New York, Inc. v. Pasquel, 187 Misc. 230, 232-233, 63 N.Y.S.2d 537 (N.Y. Sup. 1946), in which the court held that "[m]alicious attempts to induce employees to leave their employer are illegal even if there is no contract for a definite term between them and their employer and their employment is terminable at will."

In American Republic Insurance Co. v. Union Fidelity Life Insurance Co., 470 F.2d 820, 824-826 (9th Cir. 1972), the court found liability on the part of the subsequent employer where an employee "attempted to persuade nearly all of [his former employer's] sales force to follow him to [the new employer] and, in doing so, violated the duty of loyalty that he owed to [his former employer]. Sixteen salesmen accepted his offer. That is sufficient to show the requisite causality." *See also*:

Ninth Circuit: Alexander & Alexander Benefits Services, Inc. v. Benefits Brokers & Consultants, Inc., 756 F. Supp 1408 (D. Ore.1991).

Colorado: Jet Courier Service, Inc. v. Mulei, 771 P.2d 486 (Col. Sup. 1989).

Illinois: ABC Transnational Transport, Inc. v. Aeronautics Forwarders, Inc., 90 Ill. App.3d 817, 234 N.E.2d 1299 (1968).

[225]Metropolitan Opera Ass'n v. Wagner-Nichols R. Corp., 101 N.Y.S.2d 483, 492 (N.Y. Sup. 1950), *aff'd*, 279 A.D.2d 632 (1st Dep't 1951).

[226]*Id.*

[227]Cal. Bus. & Prof. Code § 17200.

nicipal, statutory, regulatory, or court-made.[228] The statute "borrows" violations of other laws and treats them as unlawful practices independently actionable under the provision.[229] It is not even necessary that the other law provide for private civil enforcement.[230] An "unfair" practice under the statute is "any practice whose harm to the victim outweighs its benefits."[231] Moreover, a plaintiff suing under the section does not have to prove that he or she was directly harmed by the defendant's business practices. Rather "an action may be brought by any person, corporation or association or by any person acting for the interests of itself, its members or the general public."[232] The remedies or penalties under the provision are limited, however, to injunctive relief, restitutionary disgorgement (i.e. the return of money which was in the plaintiff's possession or in which it had a vested interest), and civil penalties.[233] These remedies, however, "are cumulative to each other and to the remedies or penalties available under all other laws" of California.[234]

G. Violations of Trade Secrets Acts

The California Supreme Court has held that using a law firm's confidential client list "in an improper manner 'to directly solicit clients' " and for defendant departing lawyers and their new firm's "own pecuniary gain to the detriment and damage of" their former partners constitutes a violation of the Uniform Trade Secrets Act ("USTA") as enacted in California.[235,236] Under the act, "a client list qualifies as a '[t]rade secret' if it '[d]erives independent economic

---

[228]*See* Saunders v. Superior Court Of Los Angeles County, 27 Cal. App.4th 832, 846, 33 Cal. Rptr.2d 438 (1994), a case in which the plaintiffs filed suit against a group of certified shorthand reporters and two insurance companies for unfair business practices, interference with contract and interference with prospective economic advantage.

[229]Farmers Insurance Exchange v. Superior Court, 2 Cal.4th 377, 383, 6 Cal. Rptr.2d 487, 826 P.2d 730 (1992).

[230]Saunders v. Superior Court Of Los Angeles County, 27 Cal. App.4th 832, 846, 33 Cal. Rptr.2d 438 (1994), citing Samura v. Kaiser Foundation Health Plan, Inc., 17 Cal. App.4th 1284, 1299, 22 Cal. Rptr.2d 20 (1993).

[231]Saunders v. Superior Court Of Los Angeles County, 27 Cal. App.4th 832, 846, 33 Cal. Rptr.2d 438 (1994), citing Motors, Inc. v. Times Mirror Co., 102 Cal. App.3d 735, 740, 162 Cal. Rptr. 543 (1980).

[232]Saunders v. Superior Court Of Los Angeles County, 27 Cal. App.4th 832, 33 Cal. Rptr.2d 438. (1994).

[233]Korea Supply Co. v. Lockheed Martin Corp., 90 Cal. App.4th 902, 109 Cal. Rptr.2d 417 (2001), *reversed in part on other grounds*, 29 Cal.4th 1134, 131 Cal. Rptr.2d 29, 63 P.3d 937 (2003).

[234]Cal. Bus. & Prof. Code §§ 17203, 17205.

[235]Reeves v. Hanlon, 33 Cal.4th 1140, 17 Cal. Rptr.3d 289, 95 P.3d 513 (2004). The California UTSA is codified at Cal. Civ. Code, §§ 3426 *et seq.*

[236]The UTSA has been adopted in whole or in part by 44 states, as well as Washington D.C. The five states that have declined to enact the UTSA are Massachusetts, New Jersey, New York, North Carolina and Texas. Rowe, "When Trade Secrets Become Shackles" Fairness

value, actual or potential, from not being generally known to the public or to other persons who can obtain economic value from its disclosure or use' and '[i]s the subject of efforts that are reasonable under the circumstances to maintain its secrecy.' "[237] Misappropriation of a former employer's protected trade secret client list constitutes a violation of the UTSA.[238] Examples of misappropriation include "using the list to solicit clients" or "to otherwise attain an unfair competitive advantage."[239]

The court pointed out that the "UTSA does not forbid an individual from merely announcing a change of employment, even to clients on a protected trade secret client list," so long as no solicitation occurs.[240] This exception would be particularly applicable to the legal profession given the strong policies of client choice. However, the exception does not protect uses that amount to solicitation or are otherwise improper.[241]

H. Defamation

Both individuals and business entities can be defamed and sue for recovery.[242] Thus, a claim may arise when a former firm publishes defamatory statements

---

and the Inevitable Disclosure Doctrine"7 Tul. J. Tech. & Intell. Prop. 167, 193-94 (2005); Uniform Law Commissioners, A Few Facts About The Uniform Trade Secrets Act, **http://www.nccusl.org/Update/uniformact_factsheets/uniformacts-fs-utsa.asp**

[237]*Id.*, 33 Cal.4th at 1155 (citing Cal. Civ. Code, § 3426.1(d)(1)-(2)). *See also*, Morlife, Inc. v. Perry, 56 Cal. App.4th 1514, 1520-1522, 66 Cal. Rptr.2d 731 (1997).

[238]Reeves v. Hanlon, 33 Cal.4th 1140, 17 Cal. Rptr.3d 289, 95 P.3d 513 (2004).

[239]*Id.*, 33 Cal.4th at 1155. *See also*: Morlife, Inc. v. Perry, 56 Cal. App.4th 1514, 1523, 66 Cal. Rptr.2d 731(1997), American Credit Indemnity Co. v. Sacks, 213 Cal. App.3d 622, 632-633, 262 Cal. Rptr. 92 (1989). The wrongful conduct that the *Reeves* court pointed to in support of the violation included the facts "that defendants used the data to solicit a number of plaintiffs' clients directly by telephone," "defendants' business announcement caused plaintiffs' clients, many of whom lacked fluency in English, to believe their attorney had died or his firm had gone out of business" (by making no mention of the attorney's continuing practice in the announcement), and "that plaintiffs had to conduct their own mail campaign to reassure clients their firm remained able to serve them." 95 P.3d at 522-523. Moreover, the court was troubled by the fact that the "defendants prepared and distributed their business announcement without seeking plaintiffs' input or approval" contrary to the provision of Formal Opinion the State Bar Standing Committee on Professional Responsibility and Conduct No. 1985-86 that departing attorneys should cooperate with their former employers to arrange for the issuance of a joint notice to clients.

[240]Reeves v. Hanlon, 33 Cal.4th at 1156. *See also*, American Credit Indemnity Co. v. Sacks, 213 Cal. App.3d 622, 262 Cal. Rptr. 92 (1989).

[241]Reeves v. Hanlon, 33 Cal.4th 1140, 17 Cal. Rptr.3d 289, 95 P.3d 513 (2004).

[242]*See, e.g.*:

Second Circuit: Friends of Gong v. Pacific Culture, 109 Fed. Appx. 442, 2004 WL 1792080 (2d Cir. 2004), *cert. denied*, 543 U.S. 1054 (2005).

Fourth Circuit: Southern Volkswagon, Inc. v. Centrix Financial, LLC, 357 F. Supp.2d 837, 843 (D. Md. 2005).

Seventh Circuit: Brown & Williamson Tobacco Corp. v. Jacobson, 713 F.2d 262, 269 (7th Cir. 1983).

about a departing partner after his notification of withdrawal from the firm or when a departed partner makes defamatory comments about his former firm.[243] To state a claim of defamation, a plaintiff must prove (1) a false and defamatory statement concerning himself; (2) an unprivileged publication to a third party; (3) fault amounting at least to negligence on the part of the publisher; and (4) either that the nature of the statement renders it actionable per se or that the publication caused special harm.[244]

To prove the first element of a claim for defamation, the plaintiff must show that the statement in question is false, defamatory, and made in reference to the plaintiff.[245] An actionable statement is one that tends to injure or disgrace a lawyer or law firm in his or its profession.[246] Typically these statements will take the form of suggestions that an attorney or firm is incompetent, negligent, dishonest, or unethical.[247]

Publication to a third party may be proved by showing that the defendant communicated the statement to a third party, and that the defendant's statement was not protected by an absolute or qualified privilege.[248] Generally, the absolute privileges relating to defamation are plaintiff consent, publication required by law, and publication made as a part of a judicial proceeding.[249] Qualified privileges are more varied and can include: publications meant to protect a "sufficient . . . important interest" of the third party, such as in the context of an employment reference or discussion regarding the partner's character.[250]

---

[243]The elements of proof are the same in both types of actions. *See, e.g.*, Brown & Williamson Tobacco Corp. v. Jacobson, 713 F.2d 262, 269 (7th Cir. 1983).

[244]*Restatement (Second) of Torts* § 558 (1977).

[245]*Id.*

[246]*See* 46 A.L.R.4th 326. See also, 50 Am. Jur. 2d, Libel and Slander § 122.

[247]46 A.L.R.4th 326. See:
   Kentucky: McCall v. Courier-Journal & Louisville Times Co., 623 S.W.2d 882 (Ky. 1981), *cert. denied*, 456 U.S. 975 (1982).
   Louisiana: Kosmitis v. Bailey, 685 So.2d 1177 (La. App. 1996).
   New York: Van Lengen v. Parr, 136 A.D.2d 964, 525 N.Y.S.2d 100 (4th Dep't 1988).
   North Carolina: Clark v. Brown, 99 N.C. App. 255, 393 S.E.2d 134 (1990).
   Texas: Dunnam v. Dolezal 346 S.W.2d 631 (Tex. Civ. App. 1961).

[248]Restatement (Second) of Torts § 577n (1977).

[249]2 Law of Defamation § 8:2 (2d ed.).

[250]*See*, Individual Employment Rights Manual, 515-517 (BNA 1997) (". . . 21 states have enacted legislation granting immunity to employers that give job references concerning current or former employees to their prospective employers"). See also, *Restatement (Second) of Torts* § 595, cmt. i (1977).
   See, e.g.:
   Seventh Circuit: Delloma v. Consol. Coal Co., 996 F.2d 168 (7th Cir. 1993).
   District of Columbia: Wallace v. Skadden, Arps, Slate, Meagher & Flom, 715 A.2d 873 (D.C. 1998) (finding that the defamatory implications of the firm's directive to only give discharged associate's dates of employment to prospective employers seeking a reference was protected by a qualified privilege).

If the departing attorney can prove that the former firm spoke with "malice," which is spite, ill-will, hatred or the intent to inflict harm,[251] the qualified privilege can be overcome.[252]

As to the third element—fault—a plaintiff must provide sufficient evidence to show that the defendant "knows that the statement is false and that it defames the other, [and either: (1)] acts in reckless disregard of these matters, or [(2)] acts negligently in failing to ascertain them."[253]

Finally, the plaintiff must prove either that the statement specially harmed him or that is it actionable in the absence of special harm. To show special harm, the plaintiff must prove that the statement was published in print, as opposed to being spoken,[254] or the publication implied that (1) the attorney committed a crime; (2) the attorney has a loathsome disease; (3) the attorney is not fit for the practice of law; or (4) the attorney engaged in sexual misconduct.[255] If a plaintiff is not able to show special harm, he can still prove that he suffered pecuniary or economic harm. The economic harm must (1) result from the conduct of someone other than the defendant, and (2) be legally caused by the defamation.[256] Thus, if an attorney can show that the defamation caused a loss of reputation significant enough to cause a measurable economic loss, he may recover for that harm.[257] For example, if a party's defamatory statements caused an attorney to lose a large client, the attorney may be able to recover if he can show a measurable amount of lost profits attributable to the loss of the client's business.

The most prominent example of a defamation claim made by a departing partner involved a press release sent by the firm after the plaintiff, a corpo-

---

Illinois: Edelman, Combs and Latturner v. Hinshaw and Culbertson, 338 Ill. App.3d 156, 167, 273 Ill. Dec. 149, 788 N.E.2d 740 (2003) (mere fact that receipients of memorandum accusing plaintiff attorneys of concealing assets from bankruptcy trustees in order to later file those claims as lucrative class action lawsuits were attorneys was insufficient to immunize defendants from liability for the communication of defamatory material under qualified privilege in absence of allegations that the communication furthered some interest of social importance); Kuwik v. Starmark Star Marketing and Admin., Inc., 156 Ill.2d 16, 188 Ill. Dec. 765, 619 N.E.2d 129 (1993).

New Jersey: Kass v. Great Coastal Exp., Inc., 152 N.J. 353, 704 A.2d 1293 (N.J. 1998).

New York: Cellamare v. Millbank, Tweed, Hadley & McCloy LLP, 2003 WL 22937683 (E.D.N.Y. 2003).

[251]*See, e.g.*, Novecon Ltd. v. Bulgarian-Am. Enter. Fund, 190 F.3d 556, 567 (D.C. Cir. 1999), *cert. denied*, 529 U.S. 1037 (2000).

[252]*Id.*

[253]*Restatement (Second) of Torts* § 580B (1977).

[254]*Id.*, at § 569.

[255]*Id.*, at § 570.

[256]*Id.*, at § 575, cmt. b.

[257]*Id.*

rate lawyer and partner of his firm, notified the firm of his intent to withdraw and join a competing firm.[258] The press release stated that the departing partner had been accused of sexual harassment during his tenure at the firm and that the firm had investigated and concluded that there was a reasonable likelihood that plaintiff had sexually harassed another employee.[259] The release also accused the plaintiff of "lacking in 'respect and integrity . . .' " and alleged a serious downturn in his productivity.[260] In the wake of this release, the plaintiff's new employer suggested that the plaintiff withdraw from his new partnership, which he did.[261] The plaintiff sued his former firm, alleging, among other claims, defamation and injurious falsehood. The former firm settled out of court for an undisclosed sum of money and agreed to publicly apologize to the plaintiff.[262]

I. Fraudulent Inducement

Fraudulent inducement can arise in the context of lateral movement either when a lawyer makes a misrepresentation as to his background or what he can bring to the table or when a firm makes promises it has no intention of keeping.

To state a claim for fraudulent inducement,[263] a plaintiff must prove (1) a misrepresentation of fact, opinion, intention or law, (2) for the purpose of inducing him to act or to refrain from action and (3) his justified reliance on the statement.[264] This type of claim may arise where a law firm lures a partner away from a partnership with false factual statements about the firm's status, profitability, future plans, or client base. If a partner can demonstrate that the law firm fraudulently induced him to leave his former firm, the law firm can be liable for any pecuniary loss caused he suffered as a result.[265]

---

[258]*See*, Jensen v. Pillsbury Winthrop, CV-02-0191966-S, Complaint, filed in Connecticut Superior Court, Stamford-Norwalk District, October 14, 2002. The complaint is available at **http://www.americanlawyer.com/pdf/101402jensen-complaint.pdf**.

[259]*See*, Lin, "Pillsbury Sued By Ex-Partner For $45 Million," New York Law Journal, (Oct. 6, 2002).

[260]*See*, Jensen v. Pillsbury Winthrop, CV-02-0191966-S, Complaint, filed in Connecticut Superior Court, Stamford-Norwalk District, October 14, 2002, ¶ 30.

[261]*See*, Kolker, "Pillsbury's Lateral Damage: Frode Jensen's move to Latham inspired a send-off he says had ruined him," Legal Times, p.1 (Feb. 10, 2003).

[262]*See* Oreskovic, "Pillsbury Settles with Frode Jensen" April 2, 2003 (available at **http://www.law.com/jsp/PubArticle.jsp?id=900005383795**).

[263]This claim is also called "fraudulent misrepresentation" or "misrepresentation."

[264]*Restatement (Second) of Torts* § 525 (1977).

[265]*Id.*, at § 525 (1977).

A statement will be deemed a misrepresentation of fact, opinion, intention, or law (the first element) when the law firm "(a) knows or believes that the matter is not as [it] represents it to be, (b) does not have the confidence in the accuracy of [the] representation that [it] states or implies, or (c) knows that [it] does not have the basis for [the] representation that [it] states or implies."[266] Further, a representation that a firm intends to take a certain action when, in fact, the firm does not intend to do so, is also considered fraudulent.[267]

To prove the second element of a claim for fraudulent inducement, a lawyer must show that the speaker had reason to believe that the lawyer would act based on the misrepresentations.[268] The *Restatement (Second) of Torts* recommends a "reasonable man" standard of proof, meaning that an attorney must show that the law firm has information from which a reasonable man would conclude that the attorney would act in reliance on the misrepresentations.[269]

A plaintiff must then prove that reliance on the false statement(s) was justified.[270] Reliance is justified where the misrepresentation relates to a matter that a reasonable person (either in the position of the attorney or in the position of the law firm making the representations) would deem "material," i.e., important and valuable in determining what course of action to take.[271]

Calculating the pecuniary loss in such cases can be difficult. Courts have taken two approaches: the "out of pocket" rule, which typically awards the plaintiff wages lost due to his leaving his former job and the "benefit of the bargain" rule, which awards the plaintiff the money he would have earned had the promised employment materialized.[272] Many courts have granted damages awards measured against the salary that the plaintiff gave up to take on the new employment opportunity.[273] An attorney attempting to prove these damages must show that the amounts requested are neither speculative nor con-

---

[266]*Id.*, at § 526 (1977).

[267]*Id.*, at § 530. See also, Graubard Mollen Dannett & Horowitz v. Moskowitz, 86 N.Y.2d 112, 629 N.Y.S.2d 1009, 1014, 653 N.E.2d 1179 (1995).

[268]*See Restatement (Second) of Torts* § 531 (1977). See also, Reisman v. KPMG Peat Marwick LLP, 57 Mass. App. 100, 109-111, 787 N.E.2d 1060 (2003).

[269]*Restatement (Second) of Torts* § 531 (1977).

[270]*Id.*, at § 537.

[271]*Id.*, at § 538.

[272]*10th Cir.:* Okland Oil Co. v. Knight, 92 Fed.Appx. 589 (10th Cir. 2003).
  California: Robinson Helicopter Co., Inc. v. Dana Corp., 34 Cal.4th 979, 22 Cal. Rptr.3d 352 (2004).
    Florida: Kind v. Gittman, 889 So.2d 87 (Fla. App. 4 Dist. 2004).
    Maryland: Goldstein v. Miles, 159 Md. App. 403, 859 A.2d 313 (2004).
    New Jersey: McConkey v. AON Corp., 354 N.J.Super. 25, 804 A.2d 572 (A.D. 2002).
    New Mexico: Register v. Roberson Const. Co., Inc., 106 N.M. 243, 741 P.2d 1364 (1987).

[273]*See, e.g.*:
  California: Toscano v. Greene Music, 124 Cal. App.4th 685, 21 Cal. Rptr.3d 732 (2004).
  Pennsylvania: Lokay v. Lehigh Valley Cooperative Farmers, Inc., 342 Pa. Super. 89, 492 A.2d 405 (1985).

tingent.[274] Lateral partners may face difficulty in meeting this standard, as their compensation can fluctuate depending on a firm's yearly productivity.

One context in which a fraudulent inducement claim can be brought against a firm is illustrated by a Second Circuit case in which a lateral environmental attorney was induced to join the firm by representations that the firm had secured a large client in need of environmental law assistance, that the firm planned to create an environmental law department, and the lateral would head it.[275] No environmental work materialized as the large client had not actually signed on to hire the firm and after almost two years of working on general litigation matters, the attorney was dismissed. She sued and the court found the firm liable for negligent misrepresentation.[276] In so doing, it noted that the plaintiff was damaged because the misrepresentations had the effect of thwarting the attorney's career objective—specializing in environmental law—by inducing her to leave her prior environmental practice and then failing to provide her with environmental work.[277]

J. Damages

1. Compensatory Damages
a. Forfeiture of Compensation

As previously discussed, under the faithless servant rule, an employee who breaches his fiduciary duty may be required to forfeit compensation earned

---

[274]*See* Toscano v. Greene Music, 124 Cal. App.4th 685, 21 Cal. Rptr.3d 732 (2004).

[275]Stewart v. Jackson & Nash, 976 F.2d 86 (2d Cir. 1992).

[276]*Id.*

[277]*Id.* at 88. In Smalley v. Dreyfus Corporation, 10 N.Y.3d 55, 853 N.Y.S.2D 270, 882 N.E.2d 882 (2008), the New York Court of Appeals declined to either adopt or reject the *Stewart* case and instead distinguished it from the claim of fraudulent inducement it was considering. In that claim, the plaintiff employees alleged that their employer falsely responded to their inquiries as to whether a merger was being considered prior to accepting employment and at various times during the four years of their employment. When the merger did ultimately occur, four years after the discussions began, the employer fired every member of the plaintiffs' group. The court held that the plaintiffs failed to state a claim, distinguishing *Stewart* as follows:

> The core of plaintiffs' claim is that they reasonably relied on no-merger promises in accepting and continuing employment with Dreyfus, and in eschewing other job opportunities. Thus, unlike *Stewart*, plaintiffs alleged no injury separate and distinct from termination of their at-will employment. [Footnote omitted]. In that the length of employment is not a material term of at-will employment, a party cannot be injured merely by the termination of the contract-neither party can be said to have reasonably relied upon the other's promise not to terminate the contract. Absent injury independent of termination, plaintiffs cannot recover damages for what is at bottom an alleged breach of contract in the guise of a tort. *Id.* at 59.

during the breach.[278] Some courts have determined that the rule applies to partners as well as employees.[279] Further, the plaintiff law firms are not required to prove causation or actual damages to collect the forfeited funds.[280]

Though forfeiture of compensation may occur, generally most courts have not been willing to extend the forfeiture rule to a disloyal partner's capital contributions or other interest in the partnership.[281] Some courts have determined that the appropriate remedy is an adjustment to the amount that the departing partner is owed under the partnership agreement based on the impact of his departure on the former firm.[282]

b. Lost Profits

The compensatory damages that are most commonly sought against a departing partner and/or an acquiring firm are lost profits. The law with respect to damages for lost profits requires (1) a showing of causation, i.e. that the lost profits were a direct result of the wrongful act, and (2) a showing that the amount of those profits are accurate to a reasonable certainty.[283] A Massachu-

---

[278]This rule requires a disloyal agent or employee to "forfeit any right to compensation for services" during the period of disloyalty. Murray v. Beard 102 N.Y. 505, 7 N.E. 553 (1886), quoted fifty years later in Lamdin v. Broadway Surface Advertising Corp., 272 N.Y. 133, 138-139, 5 N.E.2d 66 (N.Y. 1936). *See Restatement (Second) of Agency* § 469 ("agent is entitled to no compensation for conduct . . . which is a breach of his duty of loyalty").

[279]*See, e.g.*, Dowd & Dowd, Ltd. v. Gleason, 352 Ill. App.3d 365, 287 Ill. Dec. 787, 816 N.E.2d 754 (2004) (holding that departing partners could not claim a right to retain compensation earned during the period of their breach.).

[280]*Id.*

[281]*See, e.g.*, Meehan v. Shaughnessy, 404 Mass. 419, 535 N.E.2d 1255, 1263 (1989), in which the court rejected the former firm's contention that the departing partners forfeited their right to their capital contributions, their share of the dissolved partnership's profits, and six months compensation as an "extreme remedy." 404 Mass. at 438-439.

[282]Jacob v. Norris, McLaughlin & Marcus, 128 N.J. 10, 29, 607 A.2d 142, 152 (1992); 607 A.2d at 152. Similarly, the trial court in Gibbs v. Breed, Abbott & Morgan, 181 Misc.2d 346, 693 N.Y.S.2d 426 (N.Y. Co. 1999), *rev'd on other grounds*, 271 A.D.2d 180, 710 N.Y.S.2d 578, 582-583 (2000), stated: "[i]n a number of cases, it has been held that a partner whose wrong causes the dissolution of a partnership does not forfeit his entire interest but is entitled to receive it, less damages caused by the breach," citing Staszak v. Romanik, 690 F.2d 578 (6th Cir. 1982). *See also* St. James Plaza v. Notey, 95 A.D.2d 804, 463 N.Y.S.2d 523 (1983).

[283]*See,* Wolf Street Supermarkets, Inc. v. McPartland, 108 A.D.2d 25, 33, 487 N.Y.S.2d 442 (4th Dep't 1985), in which the court said: "The general rule governing the recovery of lost profits in tort cases is that damages proximately caused by the wrongful conduct of defendant may be recovered if plaintiff proves them with reasonable certainty and without speculation." Indeed, while the court noted that the proof at trial was sufficient to permit the jury to conclude that the plaintiff had suffered a loss of business due to the defendants' total conduct, it found that there were several possible causes of the damage and "the jury should have been instructed to differentiate between damage proximately linked" to each of the claimed types of conduct. *Id.*

setts court has noted that courts may impose a constructive trust on the profits which flowed from the breach of fiduciary duty.[284]

i. Definition of "Lost Profits"

Lost profits may encompass both the profits resulting from a reduction in services to an improperly solicited client and the opportunity for additional services that were lost as a result of the wrongful conduct.[285]

ii. Causation

In proving causation, there is a distinction between harm that resulted from wrongful activity, such as pre-resignation solicitation or the furnishing of confidential information, and harm that was merely the result of the departure (which was not wrongful) and/or of the loss of a defendant's unique services.[286] Only the former is recoverable; the latter is not.[287] As a result, proof of causation for loss of a client requires a showing that the "clients would have remained with the departing lawyer in spite of any improper solicitation."[288]

The burden of proving that the client's decision was not the result of any improper solicitation activities rests on the departing lawyer.[289] Proof may

---

[284]Meehan v. Shaughnessy, 404 Mass. 419, 445-446, 535 N.E.2d 1255, 1263 (1989).

[285]In Hyde Park Products Corp. v. Maximilian Learner Corp., 65 N.Y.2d 316, 491 N.Y.S.2d 302, 306, 480 N.E.2d 1084 (1985), it was alleged that there was a breach of fiduciary duty in soliciting plaintiff's customers in an effort "to wean them away from [plaintiff]" by using customer lists and records the individual defendant had copied while he was employed as a sales manager. The court set forth the standard as follows:

> "Where the loss of such a customer resulted from defendant's solicitation, plaintiffs were 'entitled to recover as damages the amount of loss sustained by [them], including opportunities for profit on the accounts diverted . . . through defendants conduct. . . . Such 'loss' would include both plaintiffs' own lost profits resulting from a reduction in sales to the listed [plaintiff's] customers during the years in which defendants improperly solicited such customers and any lost opportunities for profits during this period. Plaintiffs may show either reduced sales to a solicited customer to whom defendant sold peat moss or that the opportunity for profit on additional sales to such customer was lost by consequence of defendants' solicitation." (Citations omitted.)

[286]See, e.g., E.W. Bruno Co. v. Friedberg, 28 A.D.2d 91, 281 N.Y.S.2d 504, 506-507 (1967), in which, after noting that any recovery of lost profits must be limited to "the loss directly resulting from the defendants' wrong," the court went on to state:

> "[I]t is well to note that the resignation by defendant . . . as a sales manager was not in itself a wrongful act and that the plaintiff is not entitled to recover for a decrease in sales or a loss of profits occasioned by the loss of [defendant's] services and capabilities."

[287]Id.

[288]Hillman, "Loyalty in the Firm: A Statement of General Principles on the Duties of Partners Withdrawing from Law Firms," 55 Wash. & Lee L. Rev. 997, 1015 (1998).

[289]Meehan v. Shaughnessy, 404 Mass. 419, 535 N.E.2d 1255, 1263 (1989).

take the form of direct or circumstantial evidence.[290] Direct evidence would consist of evidence from the client regarding the lawyer's actions and the client's decisions.[291] Circumstantial evidence focuses on "whether a client freely exercised his or her right to choose" and could include "(1) who was responsible for initially attracting the client to the firm; (2) who managed the case at the firm; (3) how sophisticated the client was and whether the client made the decision with full knowledge and (4) what was the reputation and skill of the removing attorneys."[292]

Causation may be defeated by a showing that claimed damages resulted from the fact of the attorney's departure itself—which is not a wrongful act— irrespective of any solicitation or other wrongful conduct. This would be the case if the firm did not have the expertise necessary to service the needs of the client after the departure,[293] if the departing partner's services were unique,[294] or if market conditions changed.[295] For example, if the departing partner was the only tax partner in the firm and the clients who left needed tax advice, it could be argued that the lost opportunity for profit was caused by the fact that the firm had only one tax partner and not by the solicitation.[296] The same would be true if the departing partner was able to attract business because of his particular experience and reputation and any business that

---

[290]*Id.*

[291]The case of Dowd & Dowd, Ltd. v. Gleason, 352 Ill. App.3d 365, 287 Ill. Dec. 787, 816 N.E.2d 754 (2004), illustrates how difficult this burden may be. In that case, one of the departing lawyers had been the primary person handling the account of the client at issue for thirteen years and spoke to the two client contacts on a daily basis. In contrast, the client contacts spoke with the senior partner only rarely. Both client contacts testified that they had not been solicited by the departing attorney to move their business to her new firm prior to her resignation. Moreover, the client testified that he would not have allowed the files the former firm was handling to remain there absent the departing partner. Even in the face of this testimony, the appellate court affirmed the trial's findings of improper solicitation on the grounds that (1) there was no evidence that the client had ever previously indicated that its continued business relationship at the former firm was dependent on the departing attorney or that it was in any way dissatisfied with the services received from Dowd, (2) the "unseemly manner" in which the defendants' "purposeful interference" was committed, and (3) credibility assessments within the purview of the trial court.

[292]Meehan v. Shaughnessy, 404 Mass. 419, 443-44, 535 N.E.2d 1255, 1263 (1989).

[293]*See, e.g.*, Meteor Industries, Inc. v. Metalloy Industries, Inc., 149 A.D.2d 483, 539 N.Y.S.2d 972 (1989) (no damages awarded because the plaintiff did not have the expertise to handle the business after the employee's departure).

[294]*See, e.g.*, E.W. Bruno Co. v. Friedberg, 28 A.D.2d 91, 281 N.Y.S.2d 504 (1967) (any claim for lost profits cannot encompass any profits attributable to the loss of a defendant's unique services).

[295]*See, e.g.*, Hyde Park Products Corp. v. Maximilian Learner Corp., 65 N.Y.2d 316, 491 N.Y.S.2d 302, 480 N.E.2d 1084 (1985) (one of the methods to defeat causation is by showing that plaintiffs could not have fulfilled the orders diverted by them because of the unavailability of the product and thus that the "lost opportunity for profit" was not caused by their solicitation.

[296]Meteor Industries, Inc. v. Metalloy Industries, Inc., 149 A.D.2d 483, 539 N.Y.S.2d 972 (1989).

was lost was due to the fact that he was no longer with the firm and not as a result of any wrongful conduct.[297] Similarly, any downturn in business due to the fact that the area of practice or the client's business was affected by market or other outside factors would not be compensable.[298]

iii. Reasonable Certainty

It is generally the rule that a plaintiff must establish (1) that it suffered a loss of profit with certainty and (2) the amount of those lost profits with reasonable certainty.[299] Once it is established, however, that the defendants' wrongful conduct caused the termination of the client relationship, the mere fact the relationship could or even would likely have been terminated in any event has been held not to be a basis to deem the award uncertain or speculative.[300] In this respect, the Second Circuit rejected an argument that damages could not be awarded because the wrongfully terminated agreement was terminable on 30 days notice and affirmed an award of damages projected over a five-year period in light of the plaintiff's "typically long standing relations with its clients" and the lack of evidence that the agreement would have been terminated absent the wrongful conduct.[301]

In the law firm context, one court affirmed an award of two years of lost profits notwithstanding the client's testimony that it would not have continued to use the firm absent the departing partner.[302] The court essentially concluded that the client's testimony was "closer to speculation than fact" because the defendants' wrongful activities interfered with the former firm's ability to compete.[303]

---

[297]E.W. Bruno Co. v. Friedberg, 28 A.D.2d 91, 281 N.Y.S.2d 504 (1967).

[298]Hyde Park Products Corp. v. Maximilian Learner Corp., 65 N.Y.2d 316, 491 N.Y.S.2d 302, 480 N.E.2d 1084 (1985).

[299]S & K Sales Co. v. Nike, Inc., 816 F.2d 843, 847-848 (2d Cir. 1987); Friedman, Clark & Shapiro, Inc. v. Greenberg, Grant & Richards, Inc., 2001 Tex. App. LEXIS 6525; 2001-2 Trade Cas. (CCH) P73,510 (Ct. App. 2001); Frederick D. Harris, M.D., Inc. v. Univ. Hosps., 2002 Ohio 983 (Ohio App. 2002).

[300]S & K Sales Co. v. Nike, Inc., 816 F.2d 843 (2d Cir. 1987).

[301]Id., 818 F.2d at 847-848.

[302]Dowd & Dowd, Ltd. v. Gleason, 352 Ill. App.3d 365, 287 Ill. Dec. 787, 816 N.E.2d 754 (2004).

[303]Id., 352 Ill. App.3d at 383.

> "There was no evidence introduced, for example, that Dowd was given any time to attempt to salvage its long-standing business relationship. If given the opportunity, Allstate [the client] may have remained with Dowd if offered more attractive fee arrangements (no fees for research, no second chairs at trial, and lower hourly rates are usually accorded government bodies). The latter, in the long run, might have proven more appealing to this insurer than simply having only [the departing attorney] in charge of their files. However, due to the secretiveness and abruptness of defendants' ultimate departure, the securing of the client's business was a feat accomplished at least by January 1, if not months earlier as the

Ultimately, the determination as to whether the damages sought are reasonably certain is an issue of fact which will rest on the quality of the expert analysis and testimony and the information on which it is based.[304]

2. Punitive Damages

Punitive damages may be available for claims of breach of fiduciary duty,[305] aiding and abetting breach of fiduciary duty,[306] tortious interference with contract,[307] and tortious interference based on conduct that involves malice, oppression, wanton or reckless disregard of plaintiff's rights, or other circumstances of aggravation.[308] The availability and standard for punitive damages varies from state to state but are most likely to impose them when multiple and intentional violations of fiduciary duties have occurred and the conduct was done with the intent to severely cripple or cause the maximum damage to a plaintiff's business.[309]

---

trial court believed. This alone represents some interference with Dowd's legitimate business expectation vis-a-vis Allstate and more importantly, casts doubt on how free and unfettered Allstate's decision to leave Dowd really was, absent a viable and familiar alternative (continuing to do business with Dowd at more advantageous terms). It also renders the pronouncements of Riley and Crim [the client's representatives], as the trial court said, closer to speculation than fact, as they insist. The lost profits totaled $871,199.75. Lundy [the damage expert] testified that he used a two-year period for the lost profits because of the manner in which law firms perform their accounting and because the information provided to [a bank] by defendants for [the departing attorneys' new firm's] line of credit included a two-year projection."

[304]*See, e.g.*, Dowd v. Dowd, 352 Ill. App.3d 365, 287 Ill. Dec. 787, 816 N.E.2d 754 (2004) (approving a damages award calculated through use of expert testimony, firm financial statements, and an expert's report.).

[305]*See, e.g.*, Schubert v. Marwell, 218 A.D.2d 693, 630 N.Y.S.2d 547 (1995).

[306]*See, e.g.*, Interpool Ltd. v. Patterson, 1994 WL 665850, *3 (S.D.N.Y.,1994); Fraternity Fund Ltd. v. Beacon Hill Asset Management, LLC 479 F.Supp.2d 349 (S.D.N.Y. 2007).

[307]*See* Cohen v. Davis, 926 F. Supp. 399 (S.D.N.Y. 1996); *New York:* Classic Appraisals Corp. v. DeSantis, 159 A.D.2d 537, 539, 552 N.Y.S.2d 402, 403 (1990); Canales v. Stuyvesant Ins. Co., 10 Misc.2d 583, 172 N.Y.S.2d 729, 733 (N.Y.C. Munic. 1958).

[308]*Second Circuit:* G.D. Searle & Co. v. Medicore Communications., Inc., 843 F. Supp. 895, 913 (S.D.N.Y. 1994) (applying New York law).
Fifth Circuit: Fury Imports, Inc. v. Shakespeare Co., 554 F.2d 1376, 1388 (5th Cir. 1977), *cert. denied* 450 U.S. 921 (1981).
State Courts:
Illinois: Stewart v. Ost, 142 Ill. App.3d 373, 376, 96 Ill. Dec. 846, 491 N.E.2d 1306 (1st Dist. 1986).
New York: Ulico Cas. Co. v. Wilson, Elser, Moskowitz, Edelman & Dicker, 865 N.Y.S.2d 14, 24 (1st Dept. 2008).

[309]*See, e.g.:*
California: Reeves v. Hanlon, 33 Cal.4th 1140, 17 Cal. Rptr.3d 289, 95 P.3d 513 (2004).
New York: Duane Jones Co. v. Burke, 306 N.Y. 172, 117 N.E.2d 237, 245 (1954).

Table of Authorities

Cases

ABC Transnational Transport, Inc. v. Aeronautics Forwarders, Inc., 90 Ill. App.3d 817, 234 N.E.2d 1299 (1968)

ABKCO Music, Inc. v. Harrisongs Music, Ltd., 722 F.2d 988 (2d Cir. 1983)

Academy of California Optometrists, Inc. v. Superior Court, 51 Cal. App.3d 999 (1975)

Adelphia Recovery Trust v. Bank of America, N.A., 2008 WL 217057 (S.D.N.Y. 2008), *adhered to on reconsideration*, 2008 WL 1959542 (S.D.N.Y. 2008)

Adler, Barish, Daniels, Levin and Creskoff v. Epstein, 482 Pa. 416, 393 A.2d 1175 (1978), *cert. denied*, 442 U.S. 907 (1979)

Aetna Casualty and Surety Co. v. Leahey Construction Co., Inc., 219 F.3d 519 (6th Cir. 2000)

A.H. Emery Co. v. Marcan Products Corp., 268 F. Supp. 289 (S.D.N.Y. 1967), *aff'd*, 389 F.2d 11 (2d Cir.), *cert. denied*, 393 U.S. 835 (1968)

Alexander & Alexander Benefits Services, Inc. v. Benefits Brokers & Consultants, Inc., 756 F. Supp 1408 (D. Ore. 1991)

Alleco Inc. v. Harry & Jeanette Weinberg Found., Inc., 340 Md. 176, 665 A.2d 1038 (1995)

American Credit Indemnity Co. v. Sacks, 213 Cal. App.3d 622, 262 Cal. Rptr. 92 (1989)

American League Baseball Club of New York, Inc. v. Pasquel, 187 Misc. 230, 63 N.Y.S.2d 537 (N.Y. Sup. 1946)

American Republic Insurance Co. v. Union Fidelity Life Insurance Co., 470 F.2d 820 (9th Cir. 1972)

Anesthesia Associates of Mount Kisco, LLP v. Northern Westchester Hosp. Center 2009 WL 324047, *4 (2 Dep't 2009)

Appleton v. Bondurant & Appleton, P.C., 68 Va. Cir. 208, 2005 WL 3579087 (Va. Cir. Ct. 2005)

Arthur Andersen LLP v. U.S., 544 U.S. 696, 125 S.Ct. 2129, 161 L.Ed. 2d 1008 (U.S. 2005)

A.S. Rampell, Inc. v. Hyster Co., 3 N.Y.2d 369, 165 N.Y.S.2d 475, 144 N.E.2d 371 (1957)

Estate of Janet Leigh Hough v. Estate of William Hough, 205 W. Va. 537, 519 S.E.2d 640 (1999)

Everest Investors 8 v. Whitehall Real Estate Partnership XI, 100 Cal. App.4th 1102, 123 Cal. Rptr.2d 297 (2002)

E.W. Bruno Co. v. Friedberg, 28 A.D.2d 91, 281 N.Y.S.2d 504 (1967)

Farmers Insurance Exchange v. Superior Court, 2 Cal.4th 377, 6 Cal. Rptr.2d 487, 826 P.2d 730 (1992)

Feen v. Benefit Plan Administrators, Inc., 2000 WL 1398898 (Conn. Super. 2000)

Fellhauer v. City of Geneva, 142 Ill.2d 495, 154 Ill. Dec 649, 568 N.E.2d 870 (1991)

Ferguson Transportation, Inc. v. North American Van Lines, Inc., 687 So.2d 821 (Fla. Sup. 1996)

Fliegler v. Lawrence, 361 A.2d 218 (Del. Supr. 1976)

Foley v. D'Agostino, 21 A.D.2d 60, 248 N.Y.S.2d 121 (1964)

Foster v. Churchill, 87 N.Y.2d 744, 642 N.Y.S.2d 583, 665 N.E.2d 153 (1996)

Franklin Music Co. v. American Broadcasting Cos., 616 F.2d 528 (3d Cir. 1979)

Fraternity Fund Ltd. v. Beacon Hill Asset Management, LLC, 479 F. Supp.2d 349 (S.D.N.Y. 2007)

Frederick D. Harris, M.D., Inc. v. Univ. Hosps., 2002 Ohio 983 (Ohio App. 2002)

Fred Siegel Co., L.P.A. v. Arter & Hadden, 1999 Ohio 260, 85 Ohio St.3d 171, 707 N.E.2d 853 (1999)

Friedman, Clark & Shapiro, Inc. v. Greenberg, Grant & Richards, Inc., 2001 Tex. App. LEXIS 6525; 2001-2 Trade Cas. (CCH) P73,510 (Ct. App. 2001)

Friends of Gong v. Pacific Culture, 109 Fed. Appx. 442 (2d Cir. 2004), *cert. denied*, 543 U.S. 1054 (2005)

Fury Imports, Inc. v. Shakespeare Co., 554 F.2d 1376 (5th Cir. 1977)

Future Group, II v. Nationsbank, 324 S.C. 89, 478 S.E.2d 45 (S.C. 1996)

GCM, Inc. v. Kentucky. Central Life Insurance Co., 124 N.M. 186, 947 P.2d 143 (1997)

G.D. Searle & Co. v. Medicore Communications., Inc., 843 F. Supp. 895 (S.D.N.Y. 1994)

Gibbs v. Breed, Abbott & Morgan, 181 Misc.2d 346, 693 N.Y.S.2d 426 (Sup. Ct. N.Y. 1999), *rev'd on other grounds*, 271 A.D.2d 180, 710 N.Y.S.2d 578 (1st Dep't 2000)

Gibbs v. Breed, Abbott & Morgan, 271 A.D.2d 180, 710 N.Y.S.2d 578 (1st Dep't 2000)

Goldin Assocs., L.L.C. ex rel. SmarTalk Teleservices, Inc. v. Donaldson, Lufkin & Jenrette Securities Corp., 2003 U.S. Dist. LEXIS 16798 (S.D.N.Y. 2003)

Graham v. Commissioner, 8 B.T.A. 1081 (Bd. Tax App. 1927)

Graubard Mollen Dannet & Horowitz v. Moskovitz, 86 N.Y.2d 112, 629 N.Y.S.2d. 1009, 653 N.E.2d 1179 (1995)

Groen, Laveson, Goldberg, Rubenstone v. Kancher, 362 N.J. Super. 350, 827 A.2d 1163 (2003)

Groff v. Maurice, 1993 WL 853801 (R.I Super. Ct. 1993)

Goldstein v. Miles, 159 Md. App. 403, 859 A.2d 313 (2004)

Guard-Life Corp. v. S. Parker Hardware Manufacturing Corp., 50 N.Y.2d 183, 428 N.Y.S.2d 628, 406 N.E.2d 445 (1980)

Halberstam v. Welch, 705 F.2d 472 (D.C. Cir. 1983)

Hanger v. Clifford Chance Rogers & Wells LLP, Case No. RG03120659 (2004)

Harry R. Defler Corp. v. Kleeman, 19 A.D.2d 396, 243 N.Y.S.2d 930 (1963)

Hart Enters., Inc. v. Cheshire Sanitation, Inc., 1999 WL 33117189 (D. Me. 1999)

Heick v. Bacon, 561 N.W.2d 45 (Iowa 1997)

Herman v. Coastal Corp., 348 N.J. Super. 1, 791 A.2d 238 (2002)

Hitchman Coal & Coke Co. v. Mitchell, 245 U.S. 229, 38 S.Ct. 65, 62 L.Ed. 260 (1917)

Holmes v. Young, 885 P.2d 305 (Colo. App. 1994)

Howard v. Babcock, 6 Cal. 4th 409, 863 P.2d 150 (1993)

Huber v. Taylor, 469 F.3d 67 (3d Cir. 2006)

Huffington v. Upchurch, 532 S.W.2d 576 (Tex. 1976)

Hyde Park Products Corp. v. Maximilian Learner Corp., 65 N.Y.2d 316, 491 N.Y.S.2d 302, 480 N.E.2d 1084 (1985)

Morlife, Inc. v. Perry, 56 Cal. App.4th 1514, 66 Cal. Rptr.2d 731 (1997)

Morris v. Crawford, 304 A.D.2d 1018, 757 N.Y.S.2d 383 (2003)

Motors, Inc. v. Times Mirror Co., 102 Cal. App.3d 735, 162 Cal. Rptr. 543 (1980)

Murray v. Beard, 102 N.Y. 505, 7 N.E. 553 (1886)

Multi-Channel TV Cable Co. v. Charlottesville Quality Cable Operating Company, 108 F.3d 522 (4th Cir. 1997)

Nelson v. Elway, 971 P.2d 245, 98 CJ C.A.R. 1071 (Colo. App. 1998)

Newton v. Hornblower, Inc., 224 Kan. 506, 582 P.2d 1136 (1978)

Nixon Peabody LLP v. de Senilhes, Valsamdidis, Amsallem, Jonath, Flaicher Associes, 2008 WL 4256476 (NY Sup. Monroe 2008)

Novecon Ltd. v. Bulgarian-Am. Enter. Fund, 190 F.3d 556 (D.C. Cir. 1999), *cert. denied*, 529 U.S. 1037 (2000)

Ohio Drill & Tool Co. v. Johnson, 498 F.2d 186 (6th Cir. 1974)

Okland Oil Co. v. Knight, 92 Fed. Appx. 589 (10th Cir. 2003)

Oregon: Granewich v. Harding, 329 Ore. 47, 985 P.2d 788 (1999)

Pacific Gas & Electric Co. v. Bear Stearns & Co., 50 Cal.3d 1118, 270 Cal. Rptr. 1, 791 P.2d 587 (1990)

Pepe & Hazard v. Jones, 2002 Conn. Super. Lexis 2997 (Conn. Super. Sept. 11, 2002)

Pettingell vs. Morrison, Mahoney & Miller, 426 Mass. 253, 687 N.E.2d 1237 (1997)

Pitcock v. Kasozitz, Benson, Torres & Friedman, LLP, 08 Civ. 5166 SDNY; complaint available at **http://amlawdaily.typepad.com/amlawdaily/files/jeremy_pitcock_pitcock_v.%20 Kasowitz_FINAL%20Complaint%20(pdf)-0001.PDF**

Pipher v. Burr, 1998 Del. Super. LEXIS 26, No. C.A. 96 C-08-011, 1998 WL 110135, *9-10 (Del. Super. Jan 29, 1998)

Procom Services, Inc. v. Deal, 2003 U.S. Dist. LEXIS 1956 (N.D. Tex. 1956)

Props for Today, Inc. v. Kaplan, 163 A.D.2d 177, 558 N.Y.S.2d 38 (1st Dep't 1990)

Qestec, Inc. v. Krummenacker, 367 F. Supp.2d 89 (D. Mass 2005)

Ravin, Sarasohn, Cook, Baumgarten, Fisch & Rosen, P.C. v. Lowenstein Sandler, P.C., Esx-L-6327-00 (Essex County Super. Ct., N.J.)

Reeves v. Hanlon, 33 Cal.4th 1140, 17 Cal. Rptr.3d 289, 95 P.3d 513 (2004)

Register v. Roberson Const. Co., Inc., 106 N.M. 243, 741 P.2d 1364 (1987)

Reid v. Bickel & Brewer, 1990 U.S. Dist. LEXIS 16451 (S.D.N.Y. Dec. 6, 1990)

Reisman v. KPMG Peat Marwick LLP, 57 Mass. App. 100, 787 N.E.2d 1060 (2003)

Revlon Products Corp. v. Bernstein, 204 Misc. 80, 119 N.Y.S.2d 60 (N.Y. Sup. 1953)

Richardson v. Reliance National Indemnity Co., 2000 U.S. Dist. LEXIS 2838 (N.D. Cal. 2000)

Robinson Helicopter Co., Inc. v. Dana Corp., 34 Cal.4th 979, 22 Cal. Rptr.3d 352 (2004)

S & K Sales Co. v. Nike, 816 F.2d 843 (2d Cir. 1987)

Salit v. Ruden, McKlosky, Smith, Schuster & Russell, 742 So.2d 381 (Fla. App. 1999)

Samuel M. Feinberg Testamentary Trust v. Carter, 652 F. Supp. 1066 (S.D.N.Y. 1987)

Samura v. Kaiser Foundation Health Plan, Inc., 17 Cal. App.4th 1284, 22 Cal. Rptr.2d 20 (1993)

Sanke v. Bechina, 216 Ill. App.3d 962, 160 Ill. Dec. 258, 576 N.E.2d 1212 (1991)

Saunders v. Superior Court, 27 Cal. App.4th 832, 33 Cal. Rptr.2d 438 (1994)

Sawheny v. Pioneer Hi-Bred International Inc., 93 F.3d 1401 (8th Cir. 1996)

Schubert v. Marwell, 218 A.D.2d 693, 630 N.Y.S.2d 547 (1995)

Shearson Lehman Brothers. v. Bagley, 205 A.D.2d 467, 614 N.Y.S.2d 5 (1st Dep't 1994)

Shinn v. Allen, 984 S.W.2d 308 (Tex. App. 1998)

Solow v. W. R. Grace & Co., 83 N.Y.2d 303, 610 N.Y.S.2d 128, 632 N.E.2d 437 (1994)

Southern Volkswagon, Inc. v. Centrix Financial, LLC, 357 F. Supp.2d 837 (D. Md. 2005)

Spinner v. Nutt, 417 Mass. 549, 631 N.E.2d 542 (1994)

St. James Plaza v. Notey, 95 A.D.2d 804, 463 N.Y.S.2d 523 (1983)

Stanley v. Richmond, 35 Cal. App.4th 1070, 41 Cal. Rptr.2d 768 (1995)

Staszak v. Romanik, 690 F.2d 578 (6th Cir. 1982)

Stewart v. Jackson & Nash, 976 F.2d 86 (2d Cir. 1992)

Stewart v. Ost, 142 Ill. App.3d 373, 96 Ill. Dec. 846, 491 N.E.2d 1306 (1st Dist. 1986)

Terrydale Liquidating Trust v. Barness, 611 F. Supp. 1006 (S.D.N.Y. 1984)

Tew v. Chase Manhattan Bank, N.A., 728 F. Supp. 1551 (S.D. Fla.), *amended on reconsideration*, 741 F. Supp. 220 (1990)

Toscano v. Greene Music, 124 Cal. App.4th 685, 21 Cal. Rptr.3d 732 (2004)

Trade 'N Post, L.L.C. v. World Duty Free Americas, Inc., 2001 ND 116, 628 N.W.2d 707 (2001)

Trepel v. Pontiac Osteopathic Hospital, 135 Mich. App. 361, 354 N.W.2d 341 (1984)

Ulico Cas. Co. v. Wilson, Elser, Moskowitz, Edelman & Dicker, 865 N.Y.S.2d 14, 24 (1st Dept. 2008)

United Rentals (North America), Inc. v. Keizer, 355 F.3d 399 (6th Cir 2004)

Unity House, Inc. v. North Pacific Investments, Inc., 918 F. Supp. 1384 (D. Haw. 1996)

USA Interactive v. Dow Lohnes & Albertson, P.L.L.C., 328 F. Supp.2d 1294 (M.D. Fla. 2004)

Van Lengen v. Parr, 136 A.D.2d 964, 525 N.Y.S.2d 100 (4th Dep't 1988)

Velo-Bind, Inc. v. Scheck, 485 F. Supp. 102 (S.D.N.Y. 1979)

Voyles v. Sandia Mortgage Corporation, 196 Ill.2d 288, 256 Ill. Dec. 289, 751 N.E.2d 1126 (2001)

Wallace v. Skadden, Arps, Slate, Meagher & Flom, 715 A.2d 873 (D.C. 1998)

Wal-Mart Stores, Inc. v. Sturges, 52 S.W.3d 711, 44 Tex. Sup. Ct. J. 486 (Tex. Sup. 2001)

Walters v. National Ass'n of Radiation Survivors, 473 U.S. 305, 105 S.Ct. 3180, 87 L.Ed.2d 220 (1985)

Weiser LLP v. Coopersmith, 2008 WL 2200233 (1st Dep't 2008)

Wells Fargo Bank v. Ariz. Laborers, Teamsters and Cement Masons Local No. 395 Pension Trust, 38 P.3d 12 (Ariz. 2002)

Wenzel v. Hopper & Galliher, P.C., 779 N.E.2d 30 (Ind. App. 2002)

Wenzel v. Hopper & Galliher, P.C., 830 N.E.2d 996 (Ct. App. Ind. 2005)

Wheeler v. Hurdman, 825 F.2d 257 (10th Cir. 1987), *cert. denied*, 484 U.S. 986 (1987)

White v. Kenneth Warren & Son, Ltd., 2000 WL 91920 (N.D. Ill. 2000)

Willis v. Superior Court, 112 Cal.App.3d 277, 169 Cal. Rptr. 301 (1980)

Winslow v. Brown, 125 Wis.2d 327, 371 N.W.2d 417 (1985)

Wolf Street Supermarkets, Inc. v. McPartland, 108 A.D.2d 25, 487 N.Y.S.2d 442 (4th Dep't 1985)

Yorn v. Superior Court, 90 Cal. App. 3d 669, 153 Cal. Rptr. 295 (1979)

1-800 Contacts, Inc. v. Steinberg, 107 Cal. App.4th 568 (2003)

Statutes

N.Y. Partnership Law § 105
Cal. Bus. & Prof. Code § 17200
Cal. Bus. & Prof. Code §§ 17203, 17205
Cal. Civ. Code, § 3426.1(d)(1)-(2)
Cal. Civ. Code, §§ 3426 et seq.

Rules and Regulations

Florida Rules of Prof'l Conduct 4-5.8
California Rules of Prof'l Conduct
    §§ 3-500
    §§ 3-310
I.L.C.S. S. Ct. Rules of Prof'l Conduct RPC 5.6
Mich. Comp. Laws Ann., MRPC 5.6

Md. R., Cts., J. & Attys. Rule 16-812, MRPC 5.6
N.J. R. of Prof'l Conduct R. 5.6
New York Code of Prof'l Responsibility
   DR 2-108, 22 N.Y.C.R.R. § 1200.13
   DR 5-101, 22 N.Y.C.R.R. § 1200.20
   DR 7-101, 22 N.Y.C.R.R. § 1200.32
   EC 7-8
   EC 9-2
New York Rules of Professional Conduct, Part 1200 (effective April 1, 2009)
   1.1
   1.7
   5.6

Other Authorities

ABA Comm. on Ethics and Prof'l Resp, Informal Opinion 1457 (April 29, 1980)
ABA Model Rules of Prof'l Conduct
   5.6
ABA Model Code of Prof'l Responsibility
A.L.I., Restatement (Third) of The Law Governing Lawyers § 9(3)(a), comment i
46 A.L.R.4th 326
50 Am. Jur. 2d, Libel and Slander § 122
American Law Institute, Restatement of the Law Governing Lawyers, § 26, Comment h (Tent. Draft No. 5, 1992)
Corwin, "Response to Loyalty in the Firm: A Statement of General Principles on the Duties of Partners Withdrawing from Law Firms," 55 Wash. & Lee L. Rev. 1055 (1998)
Fall 2004 National Association of Legal Search Consultants Conference Report
Gottlieb, "Suit Over Firm's Collapse Tests Limits Of Poaching Lawyers," New Jersey Law Journal, February 3, 2009
Hazard and Hodes, "The Law Governing Lawyers" § 5.6:202 (1998)
Hillman, "Loyalty in the Firm: A Statement of General Principles on the Duties of Partners Withdrawing from Law Firms" 55 Wash. & Lee L. Rev. 997 (1998)
Hillman, "The Property Wars of Law Firms: Of Client Lists, Trade Secrets and the Fiduciary Duties of Law Partners" 30 Fla. St. U. L. Rev. 767 (2003)
Individual Employment Rights Manual, 515-517 (BNA 1997)
Joint Phila. And Pa. Bar Association Ethics Op. 99-100 (April 1999)
Kolker, "Pillsbury's Lateral Damage: Frode Jensen's move to Latham inspired a send-off he says had ruined him," Legal Times, p.1 (Feb. 10, 2003)
Krauss, "Validity of Nonsolicitation Pacts Among Lawyers Shrinks," New York Law Journal, October 21, 2008, p. 4, col. 4
Law360, "NJ Case Could Test Limits Of 'Partner Poaching,' " February 3, 2009 (available at **http://www.law360.com/articles/85750**)
Oreskovic, "Pillsbury Settles with Frode Jensen" April 2, 2003 (available at **http://www.law.com/jsp/PubArticle.jsp?id=900005383795**)
2 Law of Defamation § 8:2 (2d ed.)
Lin, "Pillsbury Sued By Ex-Partner For $45 Million," New York Law Journal, (Oct. 6, 2002)
Restatement (Second) of Agency § 469
Restatement (Second) Of Torts
   § 525
   § 526
   § 530
   § 531

§ 558

§ 577n

§ 595

§ 766B

§ 767

§ 874

§ 876(b)

Rowe, "When Trade Secrets Become Shackles" Fairness and the Inevitable Disclosure Doctrine" 7 Tul. J. Tech. & Intell. Prop. 167, 193-94 (2005)

Sandburg, "Loss Not Too Pricey For Brobeck, Pole," The Legal Intelligencer, Vol. 228; No. 98; pg. 4 (May 21, 2003)

Sandberg, "Records Reveal Financial Life of Brobeck Before Its Collapse," New York Law Journal, December 26, 2003, p. 16

Sperber, "When Nondisclosure Becomes Misrepresentation: Shaping Employer Liability for Incomplete Job References," 32 U.S.F. L. Rev. 405 (1998)

The PACER (Public Access to Court Electronic Records) system

The State Bar of California Standing Committee on Prof. Resp. and Conduct, Formal Op. 1985-86

Thomas, "Called to Account," Time Magazine, June 18, 2002

Uniform Law Commissioners, A Few Facts About The Uniform Trade Secrets Act, **http://www.nccusl.org/Update/uniformact_factsheets/uniformacts-fs-utsa.asp**

Willis, "Annual Survey Of South Carolina Law: Tort Law to (b) or Not to (b): The Future of Aider and Abettor Liability in South Carolina" 51 S.C. L. Rev. 1045 (2000)

www.searchsystems.net

Index

Selected Books from . . .
THE ABA LAW PRACTICE MANAGEMENT SECTION

The Lawyer's Guide to Increasing Revenue:
Unlocking the Profit Potential in Your Firm
By Arthur G. Greene

If you are ready to look beyond cost-cutting and short-term solutions, and toward new revenue opportunities, then *The Lawyer's Guide to Increasing Revenue* will show you how you can achieve growth using the resources you already have at your firm. Discover the factors that affect your law firm's revenue production, how to evaluate them, and how to take specific action steps designed to increase your returns. The book will also show you how to fully develop your plans into a multi-year strategy for improved long-term financial results.

Paralegals, Profitability, and the
Future of Your Law Practice
By Arthur G. Greene and Therese A. Cannon

Effectively integrate paralegals into your practice, and expand their roles to ensure your firm is successful in the next decade with this essential resource. If you're not currently using paralegals, you'll learn why you need them and how to create and implement a successful paralegal model in your practice. If you're already using paralegals, you'll learn how to ensure your paralegal program is structured properly, runs effectively, and continually contributes to your bottom line. Valuable appendices contain sample job descriptions, model guidelines, confidentiality agreements, performance evaluations, and other useful resources, also provided on the accompanying CD-ROM for ease in implementation!

Results-Oriented Financial Management:
A Step-By-Step Guide to Law Firm Profitability,
Second Edition
By John G. Iezzi, CPA

This hands-on, how-to book will assist managing partners, law firm managers, and law firm accountants by providing them with the budgeting and financial knowledge they need to need to make the critical decisions. Whether you're a financial novice or veteran manager, this book will help you examine every facet of your financial affairs from cash flow and budget creation to billing and compensation. Also included with the book are valuable financial models on CD-ROM allowing you to compute profitability and determine budgets by inputting your own data. The appendix contains useful forms and examples from lawyers who have actually implemented alternative billing methods at their firms.

LawPracticeManagementSection
MARKETING • MANAGEMENT • TECHNOLOGY • FINANCE

Collecting Your Fee:
Getting Paid From Intake to Invoice.
By Edward Poll

This practical and user-friendly guide provides you with proven strategies and sound advice that will make the process of collecting your fees simpler, easier, and more effective! This handy resource provides you with the framework around which to structure your collection efforts. You'll learn how you can streamline your billing and collection process by hiring the appropriate staff, establishing strong client relationships from the start, and issuing client-friendly invoices. In addition, you'll benefit from the strategies to use when the client fails to pay the bill on time and what you need to do to get paid when all else fails. Also included is a CD-ROM with sample forms, letters, agreements, and more for you to customize to your own practice needs.

Compensation Plans for Law Firms, Fourth Edition
By James D. Cotterman, Altman Weil, Inc.

This newly updated fourth edition of *Compensation Plans for Law Firms* examines the continually evolving compensation landscape and the concepts that will affect your law firm most. You'll take an extensive look at the world of law firm compensation, including:

- Compensation theory
- The art and science of compensation
- Partner and shareholder compensation
- Of Counsel compensation
- Associate compensation
- Paralegal compensation
- Staff compensation
- Bonuses, increases, and incentives
- Debt, taxes, retirement, and withdrawal
- Evaluations, fairness and flexibility
- . . . and much more!

Risk Management: Survival Tools for Law Firms,
Second Edition
By Anthony E. Davis and Peter R. Jarvis

This book helps your firm establish solid policies, procedures, and systems to minimize risk. This completely revised edition and accompanying CD provides a comprehensive overview of risk management, offers a practical approach to risk management evaluation, and steps to take to create a "best practice" plan. Using a practical self-audit tool, the book enables lawyers to consider how well their firms are addressing each of the key components of effective risk management.

The Essential Formbook:
Comprehensive Management Tools for Lawyers
Volume I: Partnership and Organizational
Agreements/Client Intake and Fee Agreements
Volume II: Human Resources/
Fees, Billing, and Collection
Volume III: Calendar and File Management/
Law Firm Financial Analysis
Volume IV: Disaster Planning and Recovery/
Risk Management and Professional Liability Insurance
By Gary A. Munneke and Anthony E. Davis
Useful to legal practitioners of all specialties and
sizes, these volumes will help you establish profitable,
affirmative client relationships so you can avoid
unnecessary risks associated with malpractice and
disciplinary complaints. And, with all the forms available on CD-ROM, it's easy to modify them to match
your specific needs. Visit our Web site at www.law
practice.org/catalog/511-0424 for more information
about this invaluable resource.

The Lawyer's Guide to Strategic Planning:
Defining, Setting, and Achieving Your Firm's Goals
By Thomas C. Grella and Michael L. Hudkins
This practice-building resource is your guide to planning dynamic strategic plans and implementing them
at your firm. You'll learn about the actual planning
process and how to establish goals in key planning
areas such as law firm governance, competition, open-
ing a new office, financial management, technology,
marketing and competitive intelligence, client development and retention, and more. The accompanying CD-
ROM contains a wealth of policies, statements, and
other sample documents. If you're serious about
improving the way your firm works, increasing productivity, making better decisions, and setting your firm
on the right course—this is the resource you need.

Managing Partner 101: A Guide to Successful Law
Firm Leadership, Second Edition
By Lawrence G. Green
Typically, lawyer managers in a firm have few, if any,
opportunities for formal management training. The
leaders in a law firm all too often lack the education in
finance, ethics, and leadership they need to run a business. *Managing Partner 101: A Leadership Guide for*
Building the Successful Law Firm, offers suggestions,
tips, and the basic ground rules for any lawyers who
must manage other lawyers.

Winning Alternatives to the Billable Hour:
Strategies that Work, Third Edition
By Mark A. Robertson and James A. Calloway
Your entire practice is based on doing battle for your
clients. Unfortunately, the issues that arise when it
comes to assessing the value of these protective and
beneficial services are a source of contention for both
yourself and your clients. This newly revised third edition of the highly acclaimed *Winning Alternatives to the*
Billable Hour: Strategies that Work, provides you with
tools you can use in your practice to implement and
evaluate alternative billing methods, including real
case studies of lawyers and firms successfully using
alternative billing to deliver value to both the client
and the lawyer.

The ABA Guide to Lawyer Trust Accounts
By Jay G Foonberg
Avoid the pitfalls of trust account rules violations!
Designed as a self-study course or as seminar materials, with short, stand-alone chapters that walk you
through the procedures of client trust accounting.
This indispensable reference outlines the history of
applicable ethics rules; how you could inadvertently
be violating those rules; ways to work with your
banker and accountant to set up the office systems
you need; numerous forms that you can adapt for
your office (including self-tests for seminars and CLE
credits); plus Foonberg's "10 rules of good trust
account procedures" and "10 steps to good trust
account records"—intended to work with whatever
local rules your state mandates.

The Lawyer's Guide to Governing Your Firm
By Arthur G. Greene
Good governance and a positive culture in a law firm
go hand in hand. It is difficult to find a law firm that
has achieved success without having a superior culture, one that creates the best work environment and
helps everyone succeed. This new guide is a practical
and valuable resource for those firms that want to
provide better client service, as well as improve the
working environment for both lawyers and staff. It provides strategies to change the culture of the law firm,
boost morale, and effectively and efficiently manage
and govern the firm.

30-Day Risk-Free Order Form
Call Today! 1-800-285-2221
Monday–Friday, 7:30 AM – 5:30 PM, Central Time

Qty	Title	LPM Price	Regular Price	Total
_____	ABA Guide to Lawyer Trust Accounts (5110374)	$ 69.95	$ 79.95	$_____
_____	Managing Partner 101: A Guide to Successful Law Firm Leadership, Second Edition (5110451)	44.95	49.95	$_____
_____	Collecting Your Fee: Getting Paid From Intake to Invoice (5110490)	69.95	79.95	$_____
_____	The Essential Formbook, Volume I (5110424V1)	169.95	199.95	$_____
_____	The Essential Formbook, Volume II (5110424V2)	169.95	199.95	$_____
_____	The Essential Formbook, Volume III (5110424V3)	169.95	199.95	$_____
_____	The Essential Formbook, Volume IV (5110424V4)	169.95	199.95	$_____
_____	The Lawyer's Guide to Increasing Revenue: Unlocking the Profit Potential in Your Firm (5110521)	59.95	79.95	$_____
_____	Compensation Plans for Law Firms, Fourth Edition (5110507)	79.95	94.95	$_____
_____	The Lawyer's Guide to Governing Your Firm (5110684)	89.95	129.95	$_____
_____	The Lawyer's Guide to Strategic Planning (5110520)	59.95	79.95	$_____
_____	Paralegals, Profitability, and the Future of Your Law Practice (5110491)	59.95	69.95	$_____
_____	Results-Oriented Financial Management, Second Edition (5110493)	89.95	99.95	$_____
_____	Winning Alternatives to the Billable Hour: Strategies that Work, Third Edition (5110660)	74.95	99.95	$_____
_____	Risk Management: Survival Tools for Law Firms, Second Edition (5110653)	79.95	89.95	$_____

*Postage and Handling	
$10.00 to $24.99	$5.95
$25.00 to $49.99	$9.95
$50.00 to $99.99	$12.95
$100.00 to $349.99	$17.95
$350 to $499.99	$24.95

**Tax
DC residents add 5.75%
IL residents add 9.00%

*Postage and Handling $_____
**Tax $_____
TOTAL $_____

PAYMENT

❑ Check enclosed (to the ABA)

❑ Visa   ❑ MasterCard   ❑ American Express

_____
Account Number   Exp. Date   Signature

Name _____ Firm _____
Address _____
City _____ State _____ Zip _____
Phone Number _____ E-Mail Address _____

Note: E-Mail address is required if ordering the
The Lawyer's Guide to Fact Finding on the Internet
E-mail Newsletter (5110498)

Guarantee
If—for any reason—you are not satisfied with your purchase, you may
return it within 30 days of receipt for a complete refund of the price of the
book(s). No questions asked!

Mail: ABA Publication Orders, P.O. Box 10892, Chicago, Illinois 60610-0892
♦ Phone: 1-800-285-2221 ♦ FAX: 312-988-5568

E-Mail: abasvcctr@abanet.org ♦ Internet: http://www.lawpractice.org/catalog

Are You in Your Element?

Tap into the Resources of the ABA Law Practice Management Section

ABA Law Practice Management Section Membership Benefits

The ABA Law Practice Management Section (LPM) is a professional membership organization of the American Bar Association that helps lawyers and other legal professionals with the business of practicing law. LPM focuses on providing information and resources in the core areas of marketing, management, technology, and finance through its award-winning magazine, teleconference series, Webzine, educational programs (CLE), Web site, and publishing division. For more than thirty years, LPM has established itself as a leader within the ABA and the profession-at-large by producing the world's largest legal technology conference (ABA TECHSHOW®) each year. In addition, LPM's publishing program is one of the largest in the ABA, with more than eighty-five titles in print.

In addition to significant book discounts, LPM Section membership offers these benefits:

ABA TECHSHOW
Membership includes a $100 discount to ABA TECHSHOW, the world's largest legal technology conference & expo!

Teleconference Series
Convenient, monthly CLE teleconferences on hot topics in marketing, management, technology and finance. Access educational opportunities from the comfort of your office chair – today's practical way to earn CLE credits!

Law Practice Magazine
Eight issues of our award-winning *Law Practice* magazine, full of insightful articles and practical tips on Marketing/Client Development, Practice Management, Legal Technology, and Finance.

LAW|PRACTICE
THE BUSINESS OF PRACTICING LAW

Law Practice Today
LPM's unique Web-based magazine covers all the hot topics in law practice management today — identify current issues, face today's challenges, find solutions quickly. Visit www.lawpracticetoday.org.

Law Practice TODAY

LAW TECHNOLOGY TODAY

Law Technology Today
LPM's newest Webzine focuses on legal technology issues in law practice management — covering a broad spectrum of the technology, tools, strategies and their implementation to help lawyers build a successful practice. Visit www.lawtechnologytoday.org.

LawPractice.news
Monthly news and information from the ABA Law Practice Management Section

LawPractice.news
Brings Section news, educational opportunities, book releases, and special offers to members via e-mail each month.

To learn more about the ABA Law Practice Management Section, visit www.lawpractice.org or call 1-800-285-2221.

MARKETING • MANAGEMENT • TECHNOLOGY • FINANCE

LAW PRACTICE MANAGEMENT SECTION
MARKETING • MANAGEMENT • TECHNOLOGY • FINANCE